Indian Harvests

WILLIAM C. GRIMM

Indian Harvests

illustrated by Ronald Himler

McGraw-Hill Book Company

NEW YORK   ST. LOUIS   SAN FRANCISCO   DÜSSELDORF
JOHANNESBURG   KUALA   LUMPUR   LONDON   MEXICO
MONTREAL   NEW DELHI   PANAMA   RIO DE JANEIRO
SINGAPORE   SYDNEY   TORONTO

Library of Congress Cataloging in Publication Data

Grimm, William Carey, date
  Indian harvests.

  SUMMARY: Describes the major plants used by
the American Indian: strawberries, chestnuts, arrowroot, and others.
  1. Indians of North America—Food—Juvenile lit-
erature. [1. Indians of North America—Food]
I. Himler, Ronald, illus. II. Title.
E98.F7G74   970.1   72–13295
ISBN 0–07–024839–7
ISBN 0–07–024840–0 (lib. bdg.)

Table of Contents

Indian Harvests

Long *before the first Europeans came to the*
New World, many of the American Indians
cultivated food plants such as maize (Indian
corn), beans, squash, and peppers. The In-
dians were America's first farmers. However,
they also used many wild plants for food, medi-
cine, dyes, and even charms.

This book is about the food plants which the
Indians found in nature's larder. Since it would
be impossible to cover all of them in a book of
this size, only the major ones and a few that are
of lesser importance, but which are common and
well-known plants, could be included. Some of
the wild plants such as the dandelion, water
cress, and winter cresses, which many people
gather and use today, will not be found here.
They are plants of European origin, so obviously
they were not available to the Indians of primi-
tive America.

At one time or another we have all eaten
some of these Indian foods. While on hikes or
camping trips most boys and girls have enjoyed
wild berries—strawberries, blackberries, rasp-
berries, and blueberries. Every one of us has
eaten some of the nuts you will read about in
this book. Many of us have even had the pleasure

of going "nutting" in the fall, just as the Indian children did long ago. And who has not eaten cranberry sauce with the turkey dinner on Thanksgiving or Christmas?

Those who would like to learn more about edible wild plants should consult some of the books listed on page 121. Perhaps you will want to try some of the Indian foods about which you will read in the following pages. If so, a word of caution will not be amiss. It is quite easy to mistake some very poisonous plants for those that are safe to eat. This is especially true of the plants belonging to the lily and carrot families. Unless you have had some experience in field botany and are certain that a given plant is harmless, it will be best to leave it alone. Always be sure before you eat.

Ferns of many kinds grew profusely in most of the forests of primitive America. In summer, after the wild flowers of spring had withered and disappeared, ferns often carpeted the ground. In moist woodlands, particularly in the mountains, they still grow abundantly, and we admire them for their beauty. So many people have admired them, dug them up and carried them away, that few ferns are now found in the woodlands close to our cities.

A fern may not seem to be a likely source of food, and not many of them are. But there are a few which the Indians, and even many people today, have found to be quite edible. No one, of course, could eat the mature fronds of ferns; but the young fronds, when they are unrolling in the spring, are eaten by peoples in many parts of the world. These young fronds are often called "fiddleheads" for they remind one of the neck of a violin, or fiddle, with the scroll at its end.

The ostrich fern (*Pteretis pensylvanica*) often grows abundantly in stream bottoms and wet woodlands across the northern United States and Canada. It is a big fern, and in summer its circles of fronds may grow to be as much as six feet tall. In spring the tender young "fiddle-

Fertile leaf

Leaflet

Ostrich Fern

Detail

Fern Fiddleheads

heads" appear in big vaselike clumps. Before they begin to unroll they are thick and succulent, and can be cooked like asparagus or snap beans.

While the ostrich fern does not grow very far to the south, the bracken or brake (*Pteridium aquilinum*) is widespread in North America. It often grows abundantly in open woodlands, old fields, and clearings. It is by far the most common and best known of all our ferns. Country people, like the Indians of old, are aware of the fact that its young fronds are edible. They must be picked before they begin to unroll—when no more than six to eight inches tall. The raw stalks are very mucilaginous, so country boys often enjoy chewing them just as they do the twigs of the slippery elm tree. When cooked, they make quite a good springtime vegetable.

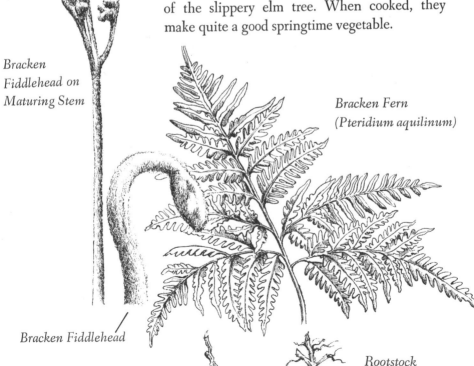

Bracken Fiddlehead on Maturing Stem

Bracken Fern (Pteridium aquilinum)

Bracken Fiddlehead

Rootstock

The Cycad Family

FLORIDA ARROWROOT (*Zamia floridana*)

Ages ago, while the great dinosaurs still roamed the earth, plants of the cycad family grew in great abundance. Now they are of minor importance in the plant world. The Florida arrowroot is one of the few cycads that has survived to the present day.

Like other cycads, the Florida arrowroot has feathery-looking, palmlike leaves that grow in a large circle close to the ground. Instead of having flowers, the plants produce a cone in the center of the circle of leaves. Some of the plants have male cones which produce pollen. Others have female cones which persist for some time and produce seeds. They are the most primitive of the living seed plants.

The large starch-filled roots of the Florida arrowroot have long been used by the Indians, and the present day Seminoles know the plant as "coontie" or "comptie." An excellent and very nutritious flour is obtained by grinding or grating the roots. The grated root is mixed with water, stirred, and then strained through a cloth. This results in a pasty mixture of starch, which is spread out on a cloth to dry and form a powdery flour. That made from the outer

Seminole Indians Processing Coontie

Root

Cone

part of the roots is pale pinkish-brown in color, but the flour made from the center of the roots is white. The flour is one of the most important foods of the Seminoles. It is used for the same purposes that we use wheat flour.

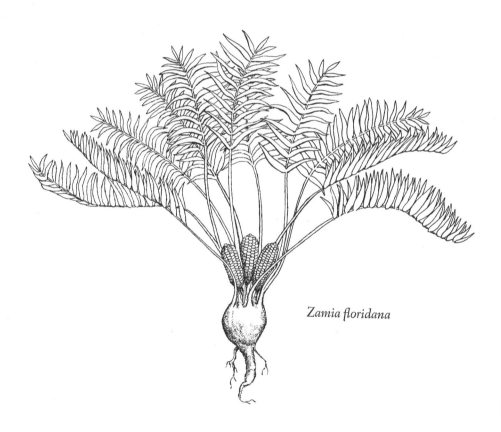

Zamia floridana

The Pine Family

Pine nuts are a primitive Indian food that a lot of people still enjoy today. These "nuts" are really the big and wingless seeds of pinyon or nut pines, the most important being the pinyon (*Pinus edulis*) and the Mexican pinyon (*Pinus cembroides*). Pinyons are rather scrubby-looking little trees which thrive on the dry foothills, gravelly mountain slopes, and canyon walls in the southwestern United States and Mexico.

We know that the seeds of these pines have long been a staple food of the Indians who dwell in the arid Southwest, for they have been found in the most ancient of Indian burial sites. Abundant crops of seeds are produced at intervals of two to five years, and the Indians still gather them in large quantities.

The Indians enjoy pine nuts both raw and roasted, for they are very palatable and have a sweet flavor. They also grind them into meal, which is used to make both bread and porridge. Today they sell large quantities of the nuts in the market for they are often the chief money crop of many of the Indians. They bake those intended for market soon after they are gathered, not only to prevent spoilage but also to preserve the fine flavor.

Markets of the Southwest sell most of the pine nuts the Indians harvest. Occasionally, customers in other sections of the country are able to buy them in their local stores. So if you can find some, this is an Indian food you should not miss.

The smaller seeds of other pines are also sweet and nutritious. They are especially good after being roasted, as roasting removes any trace of a resinous taste. These smaller pine seeds served as food for many of the Indians when other foods were scarce.

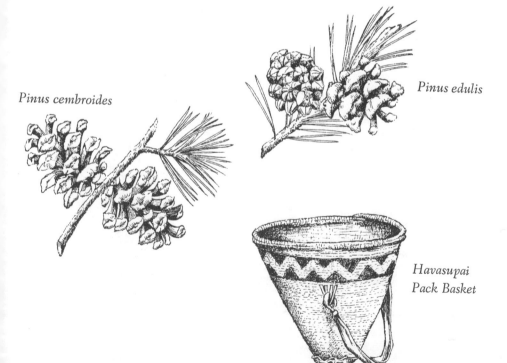

Pinus cembroides

Pinus edulis

Havasupai
Pack Basket

Many Indians also used the juicy inner bark and cambium of various pines as food. No doubt they used bark chiefly when they were hard pressed for food, but some tribes seem to have used bark quite extensively. In the Northeast the early explorers often found large areas where white pines (*Pinus strobus*) had been stripped of their bark. The name "Adirondack," which means the "tree eaters," is one that the Indians themselves bestowed upon their bark-eating kinsmen. Indians of the Northwest coastal region quite often ate the bark of the shore pine (*Pinus contorta*), while those of the Rocky Mountains occasionally used that of the ponderosa pine (*Pinus ponderosa*).

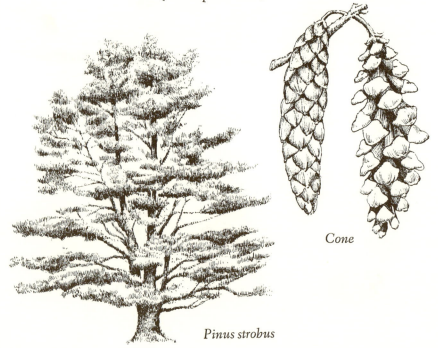

Cone

Pinus strobus

Sometimes the Indians may have eaten strips of the inner bark raw, but more often they cooked it. Very often they ground the dried bark into flour, which was used for making bread. Pine-bark bread would be most unpleasant to our taste. It was hard, very dark colored, and rather bitter. But to the Indians it was food, and no doubt it often warded off starvation.

The Indians also ate the candlelike shoots which appear on pine trees in the spring, as well as the young green cones. Many of the early New Englanders, too, ate the tender young shoots of the white pine. They candied the shoots and enjoyed them as a confection.

Cone

Pinus ponderosa

The Cattail Family

COMMON CATTAIL (*Typha latifolia*)

Any boy or girl who has spent much time outdoors is sure to be familiar with cattail plants. They are found in wet places throughout North America, except in the coldest regions. Quite likely you have played with the stalks, which are topped with sausage-shaped brown heads. When dry, in the late winter or early spring, these heads burst into fluffy masses of tiny seeds that sail away on silky parachutes.

Probably cattails never looked very appetizing to you, but the plants have always provided food for the Indians. In spring the tender young shoots, cooked as a green vegetable, were most welcome. Later in the year many of the Indians also enjoyed the young flower heads, eating

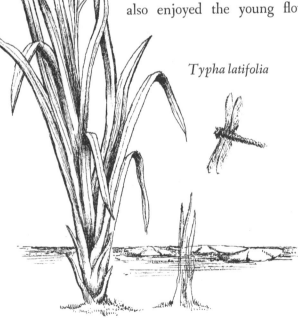

Typha latifolia

them either raw as a salad or boiled. But most important were the long, creeping rootstocks that grow in the muck. These are quite easy to pull up, and the Indians harvested them between late fall and early spring when they were full of starch. They were often boiled or baked and eaten the way we eat potatoes. The starch-filled cores were also dried and then ground into flour to be used for making bread.

The common cattail and other related species provided highly nutritious food for Indians throughout the year.

Rootstock

The Water-Plantain Family

ARROWHEADS (*Sagittaria*)

Arrowheads are among the most conspicuous plants of shallow waters. They get the name from their arrow-shaped leaves, although not all of them have leaves of this distinctive shape. During the summer they have three-petaled white flowers, which are arranged along the erect flower stalks in widely-spaced circles of three's.

Deep in the oozy mud beneath the water, some of the arrowheads produce potatolike tubers. In the fall these tubers are full of a very nutritious starch. Harvesting them, however, is usually not an easy task. Along the lower Columbia River, Lewis and Clark saw Indian women wading in water up to their waists, probing in the mud with their toes for the tubers. Sometimes the Indians obtained the tubers in a much easier way—by raiding the stores which had been gathered by industrious muskrats. Muskrats are very fond of arrowhead tubers, and the wild geese and ducks feast on them, too. Both the tubers and the plants which produce them are often called "duck-potatoes."

The Chinookan Indians called the arrowheads "wapatoo," and they were just as fond

Flowers

Sagittaria

Plant

Tuber

of the tubers as the muskrats and the wild geese and ducks. They ate them just as we do potatoes, either boiled or roasted in hot coals. Those which were not consumed immediately were boiled, cut into slices, strung on strings, and then dried in the sun for future use.

The Grass Family

WILD RICE (*Zizania aquatica*)

Wild rice is a tall grass that thrives in shallow waters. It grows from southern Canada south to the Gulf Coast, but nowhere is it found more abundantly than in the upper Mississippi Valley and the western Great Lakes region. There it forms dense stands along the streams and the margins of the lakes. For ages, legions of wild waterfowl have fattened on its seeds before making their journey south. And for time untold it has been the main food of the Indians who have lived there.

The Chippewa, the Dakotas, the Menominee, and several other tribes of Indians have always spoken of the wild rice as a special gift of the Great Spirit. Even the name of the Menominee means "The Wild Rice People," for they were so largely dependent upon this wild grain for their food.

Like the cultivated rice, wild rice grows in water, but it is quite different from the true rice. Its slender grains ripen in the late summer or early autumn. They are a dark reddish-brown to olive-brown in color and about half an inch in length. Each grain is enclosed in a husk which has a long bristle at its tip. Unlike the true rice, wild rice has defied all attempts to cultivate it. It has always been, and still is, a truly wild plant.

Before the grain is ripe, Indian women, working in pairs, go in canoes to the watery fields of wild rice. One woman in the stern poles the canoe through the dense stands. The other pulls bunches of the stalks forward and binds them together in looped bundles. This is done to protect the ripening heads from birds and to prevent the grain from being scattered by the winds. As soon as the grain ripens, it must be harvested; so the women return to the rice stands as soon as the grain is ready to harvest. This time while one poles the canoe, the other pulls the bundles over and knocks the ripened heads of grain into the canoe with a stick.

September is the "Wild-Rice Moon" and the harvest has always been a festive occasion. There is a big feast at which wild duck, fish, and freshly harvested rice are served. A prayer of thanksgiving is offered to the Great Spirit who so generously provided such wonderful food.

After the grain is harvested, it is dried in the sun, or in bark baskets or kettles over a low fire. Then comes the threshing, a task which falls to the men. It is either flailed with sticks or

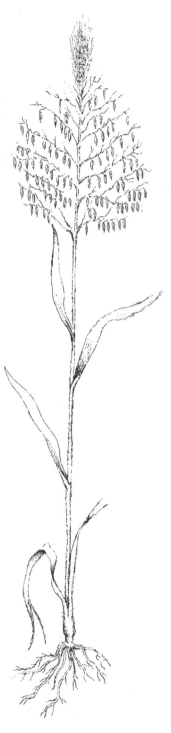

Wild Rice

Indian Women Harvesting Wild Rice

trampled with moccasined feet to loosen the grain from the husks. Next it has to be winnowed to separate the grain from the husks, and this is done by the women. The cleaned grain is stored in bark boxes or in bags made of animal skins. The Indians grind much of it into flour, which they then use for making bread. Whole grains are usually cooked with meat or used to thicken soups.

One can buy this choice Indian food in the better stores, but it is the most expensive cereal on the grocer's shelves. Many people like to serve wild rice whenever they have wild duck for dinner, just as the Indians of the wild-rice country have done for many, many years.

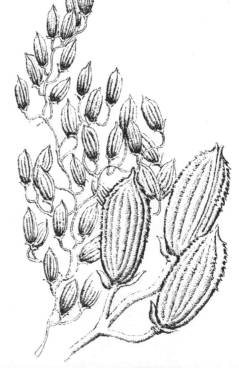

Domesticated Rice

The Sedge Family

BULRUSHES (*Scirpus*)

Bulrushes, like the cattails, are conspicuous plants in wet places across America. Some of them have round green stems, which are often several feet tall and appear to be leafless. Others have three-sided stems. The stems are tipped by small brown spikes of flowers, which usually grow in clusters.

The Indians used the rootstocks of bulrushes extensively as food. They dug them in the autumn when they were well filled with starch. Sometimes they ate them raw. More often they dried and ground them into meal which they used for making bread. The young rootstocks contain quite a bit of sugar, so they were mashed and then boiled in water to make a sweet syrup. The new shoots, which are formed on the plants in the autumn, are crisp and sweet, and the Indians frequently ate these raw.

In the southwestern United States and adjacent Mexico bulrushes grow abundantly on overflowed land. There the plants are known by the Spanish name "tule," which is pronounced *too*-lay. In California, at the junction of the Sacramento and San Joaquin rivers, large tracts are known as "tule lands."

Rootstock

Scirpus americanus

The Palm Family

CABBAGE PALMETTO (*Sabal palmetto*)

The cabbage palmetto is an impressive-looking palm for it often becomes a tree from twenty to thirty feet tall, with a crown of big fan-shaped leaves. It is the commonest tree palm throughout Florida, and it ranges up the Atlantic Coast as far as southeastern North Carolina. One frequently sees it planted about home grounds and along streets in the warmer parts of the Southeast. And both Florida and South Carolina have made it their State Tree.

Although the Indians ate the roundish, shiny black fruits of this palm, it is most famous for another food it furnished them. In the center of its crown of leaves there is a large bud which in size and general appearance resembles a head of cabbage. This palm cabbage, or swamp cabbage as it is often called, is tender and has a delicious taste. It can be eaten either raw or boiled, and it has long been one of the favorite foods of the Indians. From this big edible bud, the cabbage palmetto got its name.

Not only the Indians but a great many other people have found the palm cabbage to their liking. Sometimes these are sold in the markets and even served in restaurants. Unfortunately,

Sabal palmetto

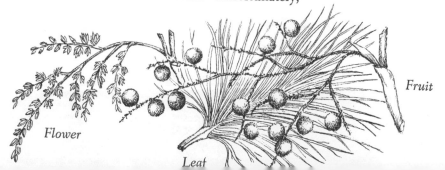

Flower

Leaf

Fruit

the removal of the bud results in the death of the tree, and it seems a shame to sacrifice a beautiful palm for a mere dish of salad or boiled palm cabbage.

SAW PALMETTO (*Serenoa repens*)

Throughout the coastal pine lands of Georgia and Florida, and westward to the Mississippi, the saw palmetto is a conspicuous and abundant plant. It is a dwarf and scrubby-looking little palm with fan-shaped leaves, and the edges of its leaf stalks are sharply toothed like a saw. In the fall the Indians gathered its oval-shaped, golden-brown and sweet fruits. They enjoyed them as much as we do cultivated dates; which, of course, are the fruits on another kind of palm.

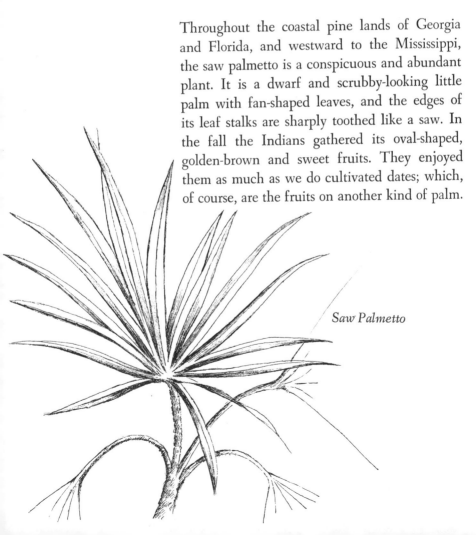

Saw Palmetto

The Arum Family

SKUNK CABBAGE (*Symplocarpus foetidus*)

Before the buds of the trees begin to swell, skunk cabbages push their shell-like spathes out of the half-frozen muck in swampy places. Within each purple-spotted and streaked hood is a thick roundish stalk which is covered with tiny flowers. Skunk-cabbage flowers do not really look very much like flowers, but they are always among the first flowers of spring.

The Indians always welcomed the appearance of the skunk-cabbage hoods. They knew that shortly they would be followed by tender green leaves, neatly rolled up in cones as they pushed their way out of the muck and water. These leaves would provide them with the season's first greens. So it is easy to imagine what a welcome sight they were.

All parts of the skunk-cabbage plants have a most unappetizing odor—quite like that given off by a skunk. Like other members of the arum family, they also contain tiny crystals of a chemical called calcium oxalate. These little needle-like crystals cause an intense stinging and burning of the mouth and throat if any part of the plant is eaten raw. To get rid of both the skunk-like odor and the fiery and puckery qualities, the

Indians boiled the leaves in several changes of water. Many people who have tried this Indian food claim that young skunk-cabbage leaves make very good boiled greens.

Sometimes the Indians also roasted the big roots of the skunk cabbage. They are full of starch, and after being roasted and dried, the roots were ground into flour for making bread. The roots, however, are very difficult to dislodge from the earth. Very few of us today would care to go to the trouble of digging them up as a source of food.

Skunk Cabbage

YELLOW-SKUNK CABBAGE (*Lysichitum americanum*)

In the western part of North America, from Alaska southward to California and Montana, Indians as eagerly awaited the appearance of the yellow skunk-cabbage spathes. Those of the western plant are a bright yellow and do not enclose the thick stalk which bears the tiny flowers. In fact, they are so attractive that the yellow skunk cabbage is sometimes grown in boggy flower gardens. The western Indians used both the leaves and the roots of this western plant in the same ways that the eastern Indians used the eastern skunk cabbage.

JACK-IN-THE-PULPIT (*Arisaema triphyllum*

Most country boys call the familiar Jack-in-the-pulpit the "Indian turnip." They take great delight in tricking an unsuspecting companion into tasting the "delicious turnip" dug from the earth at the base of the plant. It takes just one little nibble to convince the victim of the prank that he has been deceived. His mouth feels as

Spathe

Spadix

Jack-in-the-Pulpit
(Section View)

Fruit

Jack-in-the-Pulpit

Root

if he had put a hot coal into it, and he sputters and fumes as the country lad laughs at his antics.

It is true that the Indians used the peppery and puckery corms of the plant as food. But they did so only after the burning qualities had been removed by drying and boiling the corms. When properly prepared, the Indians enjoyed the mild flavor of the "turnips." Like the roots of the skunk cabbage they, too, were often dried and ground into flour for bread.

Most of us today think of the Jack-in-the-pulpit as a familiar wildflower of the spring woodlands. Jack, the little preacher, is a club-shaped stalk called a spadix. On its base are clustered tiny flowers; these later develop into a cluster of bright red berries. Jack stands in an old-fashioned covered pulpit which is a spathe. It is often handsomely striped with dark purple.

ARROW ARUM (*Peltandra virginica*)

In shallow waters and wet places from southern
Maine westward to the Great Lakes, and southward to the Gulf, the arrow arum often grows
abundantly. It has arrow-shaped leaves with
numerous veins running from the midrib to the
leaf margin. In early summer its minute flowers
are borne on a stalk within a long, slender and
leathery spathe.

Deep in the muck, the plants have big roots,
full of starch, which the Indians harvested in
the fall or early spring. They often ate them
roasted. More often, however, the roots were
dried and ground into a white flour with which
they made bread. Often, too, they ate the boiled
berries; and sometimes the big seeds within
them were dried and ground into meal.

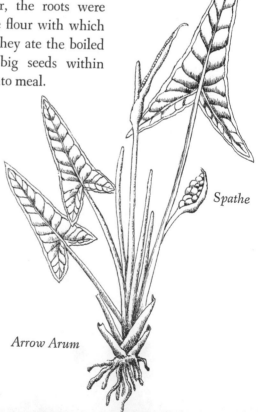

Spathe

Arrow Arum

GOLDEN CLUB (*Orontium aquaticum*)

Flower

In early spring the golden club sends up finger-like, spongy clubs from out of the dark swamp waters. Their tips are covered with tiny golden-yellow flowers; later these develop into a cluster of berries which resemble green peas. They are closely followed by satiny, oval-shaped green leaves, standing above the water or floating on its surface. When the leaves are pushed down into the water, they come back out perfectly dry, and in some parts of the South people call this plant the "never-wet."

"Tuckahoe" was a name the Leni-Lenape Indians gave to both the golden club and the arrow arum, for the roots and the seeds of both plants were prepared in the same manner.

Golden Club

CAMASS (*Camassia quamash*)

Each spring hosts of camass plants have always transformed wet meadows of the Northwest into seas of blue flowers. Such sights, or course, always gladdened the hearts of the Indians, for the starchy and nutritious bulbs of the camass were one of their chief vegetable foods.

It was only natural that they resented other Indian tribes or white settlers trespassing on their tribal camass grounds. Many a time it led to conflict and bloodshed. Camass bulbs, as a matter of fact, led to the war with the Nez Percé Indians under their famous leader Chief Joseph in 1877. It was all brought about by the decision of the Nez Percés to leave their reservation in quest of the bulbs. White settlers, too, soon discovered that the onion-shaped bulbs were delicious as well as nutritious. There were times when the members of the Lewis and Clark expedition depended entirely upon them for food.

The Indians usually baked the camass bulbs in pits lined with flat stones. A fire was made in the bottom of the pit, and after the stones became hot, the ashes were removed. The pit was then lined with green leaves and partially filled

Camass

with the bulbs. They were covered with more green leaves, then the pit was heaped over with earth. After about thirty-six hours, the earth was removed and the bulbs were taken out and eaten. Sometimes a molasses, which the Indians used on festive occasions, was made from the camass bulbs.

SEGO LILY (*Calochortus nuttallii*)

Mariposa lilies are among the most beautiful of western wildflowers. About fifty kinds of them grow in various parts of the west, and one of them is known as the sego lily. Sego lilies have pretty tuliplike flowers made up of three white petals. The base of each petal is yellow and most often marked with a crescent-shaped purple spot.

Beneath the ground the sego lily has a corm which is about the size of a walnut. It is sweet and nutritious, so sego-lily bulbs were always eagerly sought by the Indians. They often ate them raw, and they also enjoyed them after having boiled them or roasted them in the hot ashes of the campfires. Only the abundance of sego lilies made it possible for the Mormon settlers to survive their difficult early years at the Great Salt Lake. Thus the State of Utah chose the beautiful sego lily as its State Flower.

Sego Lily

WILD ONIONS AND LEEKS (*Allium*)

The onions we grow and use today are plants that came to America from the Old World, but several kinds of onions have always been present in our forests and meadows. These native wild onions were widely used by the Indians. They ate them raw as green onions, cooked them, and often used them to flavor their soups and stews. In pioneer days, the early settlers likewise made very good use of the wild onions, one of the most common and widespread being the nodding onion (*Allium cernuum*).

During the spring, you may come across plants in the Appalachian woodlands that have broad, flat, elliptical leaves and smell like onions. If you were to ask a native what these plants are, he would quickly tell you that they are "ramps"; but most of the books call them the wild leek or *Allium tricoccum*. While the leaves are present, you will look in vain for flowers, for they come later after the leaves have withered and disappeared. People who dwell among our southern mountains are very fond of the onion-reeking bulbs. And like the Indians who lived in these hills long before them, they still dig for the bulbs every spring.

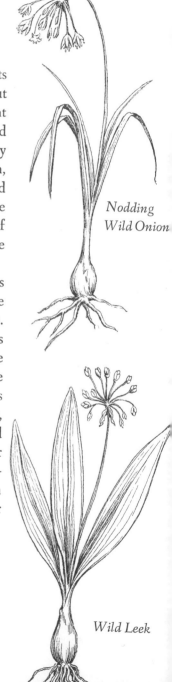

Nodding Wild Onion

Wild Leek

OTHER LILY FAMILY FOODS

In our eastern woodlands there is a little plant which has a circle of leaves about the middle of its stem. At the top there is another circle usually of three smaller leaves, and from their bases, spidery-looking flowers hang on slender stalks in the spring. Later the flowers are followed by round bluish-black berries. Well beneath the ground, this plant has a crisp, white, fleshy rootstock. It has a taste somewhat between that of a raw potato and a cucumber, so it is called the Indian cucumber root (*Medeola virginiana*). Without any doubt the Indians at least enjoyed it as a pleasant nibble.

Indian Cucumber Root

In the same woodlands one may find one of the species of Solomon's-seal (*Polygonatum*). They have leaves arranged along an arching stem; and from the places where the leaves join the stem, dangle small greenish-yellow, bell-shaped flowers. Later the flowers are followed by ball-shaped blueberries. Solomon's-seals get their name from the large round scars on their fleshy rootstocks, which mark the places where leafy stems grew in previous years. The Indians dried these rootstocks and ground them into meal for making bread. Sometimes they also used the young shoots, cooking them as a green vegetable.

The false spikenard (*Smilacina racemosa*), growing in both eastern and western woodlands, is sometimes called the false Solomon's-seal. This plant has a plumelike cluster of small white flowers at the tip of a zig-zag leafy stem. Later the flowers are followed by speckled berries, which finally become ruby red. Beneath the ground, it has a large, fragrant rootstock which was sometimes boiled and eaten by the Indians. The young shoots, like those of the Solomon's-seals, were also eaten as boiled greens.

Solomon's seal

Rootstock

Fruit

False Spikenard

Rootstock

44

A number of the true lilies (*Lilium*) are found in various parts of North America. They are among the most beautiful of our wildflowers. In many places, however, they are becoming increasingly scarce. Some of them may actually be in danger of extinction. If the flowers are picked, the plants are prevented from producing seeds; in addition, all too often the bulbs are dug up by those wishing to transplant them into their gardens.

Lilies have scaly bulbs that are both wholesome and nourishing, and the Indians often used them for making soup. No doubt lilies were much more abundant in primitive America than

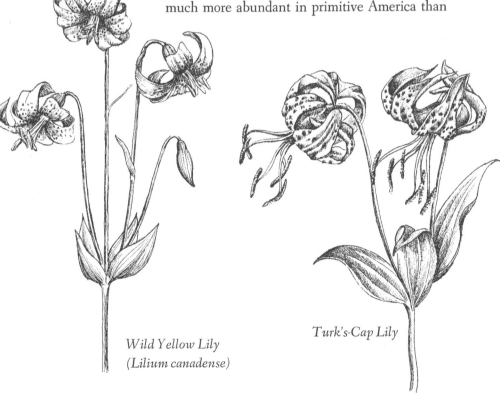

Wild Yellow Lily
(Lilium canadense)

Turk's-Cap Lily

Lilium superbum

they are today. We should not use the bulbs for food except in extreme emergency, for our wild lilies are treasured wildflowers and are definitely in need of protection.

Greenbriers are woody vines which can be recognized by their bright green and often prickly stems. One of them found quite abundantly in the Southeast is called the China brier (*Smilax bona-nox*). From its large and starch-filled roots, the Indians obtained an excellent reddish-colored flour, which they used alone or mixed with corn flour to make cakes and fritters. They also obtained a jelly by mixing the flour with warm water and sweetening it with honey.

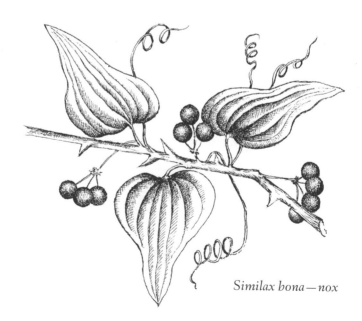

Similax bona — nox

46

The fruits or seed pods of the yuccas (*Yucca*) are still widely used by the Indians as food. Sometimes the ripe pods are eaten raw. The green ones are commonly boiled or roasted, and they are also sliced and dried in the sun for winter use. Even the young flower buds are frequently boiled and eaten, as the nectar they contain gives them a pleasantly sweet taste.

Yucca pods always have little holes in them—and for an interesting reason. Wherever the plants grow, the little white pronuba moths are also present. After the female moths lay their eggs on the pistils of the yucca flowers, they gather pollen from the anthers and deliberately place it on the stigmas of the pistils. Larvae of the pronuba moths feed upon the developing seeds. When they are grown and ready to pupate in the ground, they crawl out, leaving the little holes; but plenty of seeds are left to assure the perpetuation of the yucca plants. If it were not for the pronuba moths, the yuccas could never produce seeds, and there would likewise be no yucca fruits for the Indians to harvest.

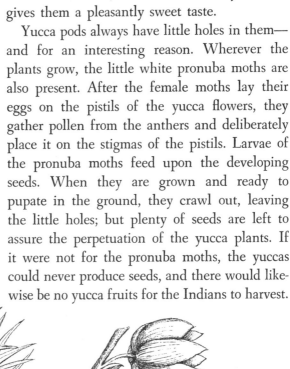

Yucca

The Amaryllis Family

AGAVE, OR CENTURY PLANTS (*Agave*)

Agaves are often called century plants for it takes the plants many years to produce the tall stalks which bear their flowers. It does not, however, take as long as a century for the plant to bear flowers, fruit, and seed. Our southwestern Indians quite generally know the agave plants as "mescal," while in Mexico they are usually called "maguey."

The cabbagelike clump of tender young leaves and the big flower bud in the center of the agave plant have long been used by the Indians as food. In the arid Southwest, agave hearts are cooked in much the same way as the Indians of the Northwest cook camass bulbs. A pit is dug in the ground and lined with stones, then a fire is built in the pit. After the stones are thoroughly heated, the ashes are raked out. Agave hearts are then placed in the pit and covered with yucca leaves or grass. The pit is refilled with earth and a fire is built over it. After cooking for a couple of days, the agave hearts are ready to be taken out and eaten.

Agave americana

Indian Children Gathering Walnuts

Autumn was always a busy time for the Indians because so many foods had to be harvested and stored for the winter. The men and the older boys were usually hunting the wapiti or elk, the bison, deer, and bear for the winter's meat supply. So the task of harvesting nuts always fell to the Indian women and children.

Indian children, like boys and girls today, always enjoyed the trips into the surrounding forests to gather nuts. The fall air was cool, crisp, and clean; the trees were gay with brightly colored leaves. It was great fun to kick aside the red, yellow, and brown leaves and find the fallen nuts beneath them.

Usually, too, they saw many of their furred and feathered neighbors who were also looking for nuts. Squirrels and jays were especially busy, gathering the nuts and burying them here and there beneath the carpet of fallen leaves. Even after snows came and covered the ground, the animals were able to find many of the nuts which they had buried and dig them up to eat. But they never found all of them, and when spring came these buried nuts sprouted and began to grow. Most of the nut-bearing trees in the forest have grown from nuts which squirrels and jays buried during autumns long past.

Black Walnut Leaf

BLACK WALNUT (*Juglans nigra*)

Ever since the days of the Indians, black walnuts have been esteemed for their distinctive taste, which is unlike that of any other nut. Most of us enjoy the strong-flavored but delicious nut meats in candies, cakes, and ice cream.

Each fall the nuts are gathered by country people and others enthusiastic about them. They are enclosed within a fleshy hull which does not split open. Removing the hulls is quite a messy job, for they contain a juice which stains one's hands a deep brown. Pioneer women used the walnut hulls to dye their homespun cloth. It is quite a task, too, to extract the fragrant oily kernels from their bony shells once the hulls have been removed. Therefore, many people today much prefer to buy their black walnut meats in the plastic bags or vacuum-sealed cans that are sold in grocery stores.

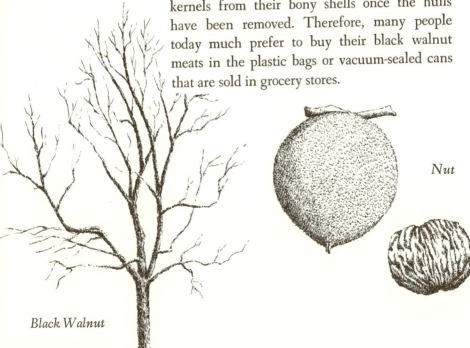

Nut

Black Walnut

BUTTERNUT (*Juglans cinerea*)

The butternut, or white walnut, also grows in our eastern forests, but its sweet and more delicately flavored nuts are much less familiar to most people than is the black walnut. The hulls which cover its narrowly egg-shaped nuts are thinner than those of the black walnut, and they are covered with sticky hairs. They, too, will stain one's hands, and in early days butternut hulls were used to dye cloth yellow or orange. The Indians prized them most highly as a source of oil for their cooking, but they also enjoyed eating the nuts.

Leaf

Nut

Butternut

52

HICKORIES (*Carya*)

Several species of hickories are found in the
eastern United States, but none of them grow in
the Far West. By far the most popular and best
known of them today is the pecan (*Carya
illinoensis*). Wild pecans grew in the Midwest,
particularly in the Mississippi Valley, but cultivated trees are now widely grown throughout
the South. Quite naturally, pecans were a great
favorite of the Indians who lived where the wild
trees grew, but the wild pecans had smaller and
thicker-shelled nuts than those of today's cultivated varieties.

In the East where the pecan does not grow,
country people still gather the nuts of the shagbark (*Carya ovata*) and other sweet-meated hickories. But in many places today, they are har-

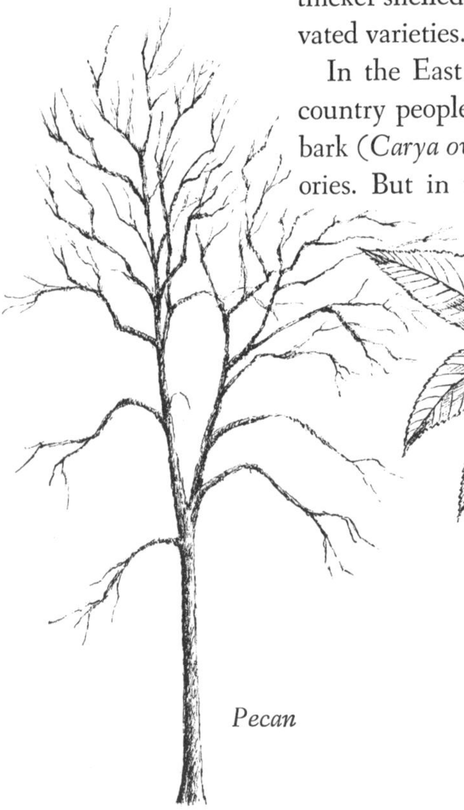

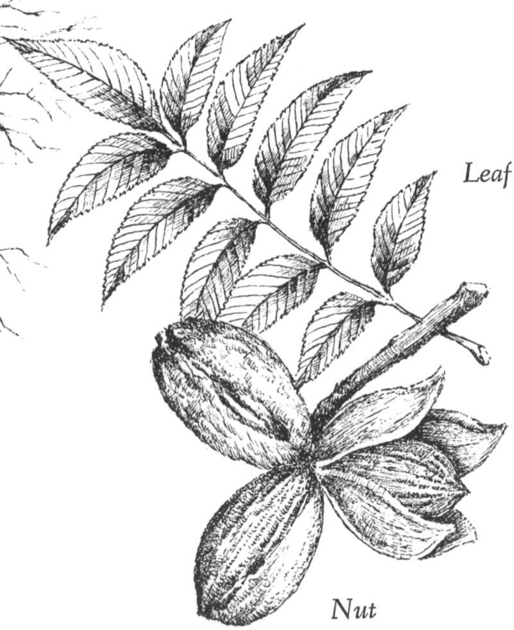

Leaf

Pecan

Nut

vested mainly by squirrels. The Indians, however, prized them very highly and gathered them in great quantities. When William Bartram traveled among the Creeks during the eighteenth century, he saw more than a hundred bushels, which belonged to a single family!

The Indians obtained a very fine oil from hickory nuts. To get it they crushed the bony-shelled nuts and boiled them in water. As the oil rose to the surface, it was skimmed off. A mass of the mashed nut meats collected in the kettle above the broken bits of shell. This was either eaten as porridge or made into cakes and dried for winter use. They also made a milky liquor, which they called "powcohiccora," by mashing the nuts in water. It was from this Indian word that our ancestors got the name hickory for these nut-bearing trees.

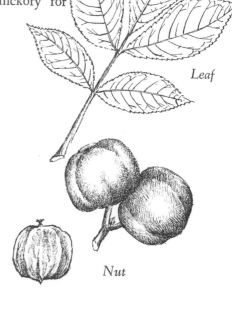

Leaf

Nut

Shagbark Hickory
(Carya ovata)

The Birch Family

HAZELNUTS (*Corylus*)

Along country roadsides, in hedgerows, and the borders of woodlands, one frequently comes across thickets of hazelnut bushes. In early spring they are especially noticeable, for then their slender branches are hung with dangling yellow catkins. These catkins are made up of stamen-bearing flowers, and they produce clouds of dusty pollen. Much less noticeable are the pistil-bearing blossoms. One has to look carefully to find them for only their blood-red stigmas protrude from scaly buds toward the tips of the branchlets.

The hazelnuts which develop from the pistil-bearing flowers come wrapped up in a pair of bracts, or modified leaves. The nuts have rather thin shells with a big scar at the bottom, and the kernels within them are sweet and delicious. Where the bushes grow abundantly, country people still gather the edible nuts in the fall. Quite often, however, the birds, squirrels, and other small animals make more use of them than man does.

The Indians always made good use of their crops of hazelnuts. They not only enjoyed eating them raw, but also ground them into a meal which made a tasty cakelike bread. Filberts, which are among the nuts commonly sold in the stores today, are nothing more than an Old World species of hazelnut.

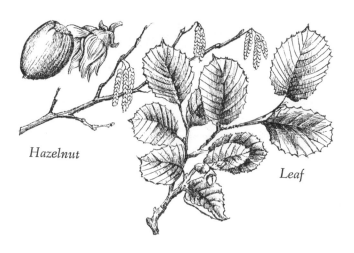

Hazelnut

Leaf

Filbert Nuts

The Beech Family

AMERICAN BEECH (*Fagus grandifolia*)

The beech is one of the most familiar of forest trees in eastern North America. It is easily recognized by the smooth gray bark of its trunk, which all too often is disfigured by carved initials. After autumn's frosts, the small and weak prickly burs open and little three-sided nuts drop to the ground. But the beech is not a very dependable nut producer. Years often pass between good crops of beechnuts.

Not many people bother to gather the sweet-meated little nuts today, but they were eagerly harvested by the Indians. From them, they pressed an oil that has been compared favorably with the finest olive oil. It could be kept for a long time and not become rancid. The Indians therefore prized beechnut oil very highly, and they used it as we use butter or cooking and salad oils.

Nuts

American Beech

Nuts and B Close-up

Leaf

AMERICAN CHESTNUT (*Castanea dentata*)

During the early part of the present century, the American chestnut grew abundantly in the forests of eastern America, and it was one of the largest and most useful of all our forest trees. It was a very reliable source of food, too, not only for the Indians but for a great many of the furred and feathered creatures of the forest. Unlike the other nut-bearing trees, the chestnut did not bloom until the danger of frosts was usually past. It was June or July when the chestnut put forth its masses of creamy-white flowers. Virtually every fall, therefore, the trees could be counted on to produce a bountiful crop of delicious nuts.

The Indians were very fond of chestnuts. They ate them raw, boiled, and roasted. Quantities of them were always ground into flour to be baked into bread. A Cherokee specialty was a dough made of corn flour and the kernels of

Leaf

Nuts

Burr

American Chestnut

chestnuts which was baked inside of cornhusks.

Today the chestnut is about gone from our forests because the great trees were killed by a fungus disease brought from abroad. In many places their bleaching trunks still stand like ghostly sentinels in the forests. Sprouts still come up from the old roots. Sometimes they even grow large enough to produce a few burs filled with nuts. But sooner or later they, too, are killed.

Fate has been kinder to the eastern chinquapins which are smaller cousins of the chestnut, for they still survive. They have smaller burs, which usually hold but a single nut, but they are sweet and almost as good as those of the chestnut. Another relative, the golden chinquapin (*Castanopsis chrysophylla*) of the Pacific Coast, is a big tree which has evergreen leaves. West Coast Indians have long enjoyed its nuts. They are much like those of the eastern chinquapins, but they require two full growing seasons to mature.

Castanopsis chrysophylla

OAKS (*Quercus*)

Oak trees produce nuts, too. They are the familiar acorns—nuts which are seated in scaly cups until they ripen and drop to the ground. Many wild creatures feast upon acorns. They are eaten by deer, bears, squirrels, wild turkeys, and many other birds and mammals. And they have always been a staple food of Indians who lived in forested regions where oak trees grew.

The Indians gathered large quantities of acorns in the fall. During the winter of 1620, the Pilgrims found baskets full of roasted acorns that the Indians had hidden in the ground. Some of the western Indians lived on them to such an extent that they were nicknamed the "acorn-eaters."

The acorns of the various white oaks were always preferred, for their pale-colored acorns were relatively sweet. The acorns of these oaks mature in the fall from flowers of the previous spring. Those of the red or black oaks require two growing seasons for their acorns to mature, and they have kernels which are yellowish and usually very bitter.

Before the Indians could use acorns as food, it was necessary to remove the bitter tannin. To do

Oak

*Pomo Indians Preparing Acorns
For Bread*

this, the shelled kernels were either dried in the sun or roasted, then they were ground into a fine meal or flour. The meal was then put into a basket, and water was allowed to flow through it. At first the tannin colored the water yellow. When it became clear, the Indian women knew that most of the bitter substance had been leached out. The doughlike mass left in the basket was then ready to be formed into loaves and baked.

Unless we were extremely hungry, the Indian's acorn bread would not be very tempting. It was heavy and pasty, since they had no yeast or baking power to make it rise. It did not look at all attractive, but it was nutritious. And the Indians at least seemed to relish it.

Leaf

Nut

The Elm Family

HACKBERRIES AND SUGARBERRIES
(Celtis)

The hackberries and sugarberries are trees or shrubs which are found in various parts of North America. Their purplish to brownish pea-sized fruits are not ready to eat until after hard frosts occur in the fall, and they may linger on the trees throughout most of the winter if they are not devoured by hungry birds.

The little fruits have a very large stone surrounded by a very thin flesh and covered by a tough dry skin. There isn't really very much in them to eat; but what little there is happens to be sugery sweet, with a taste very much like that of dates. The Indians seem to have been very fond of them, and the Dakotas often used the powdered dry pits as a seasoning when cooking meat.

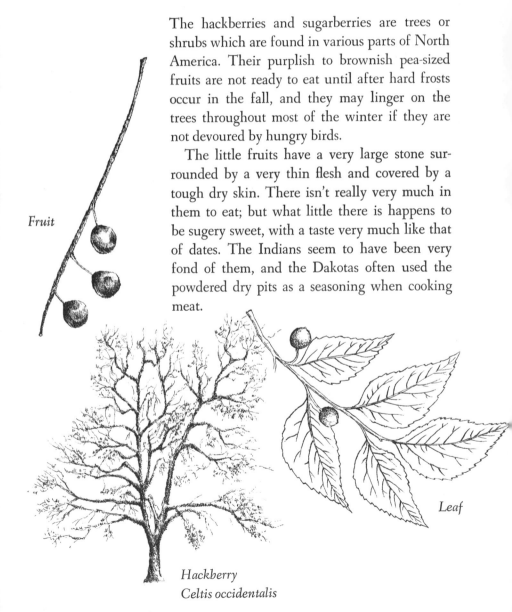

Fruit

Leaf

Hackberry
Celtis occidentalis

RED MULBERRY (*Morus rubra*)

Ripened mulberries look a lot like blackberries, but they grow on trees and they develop from little clusters of tiny flowers instead of a single blossom. When fully ripe, the dark purple fruits are sweet and juicy. They usually ripen before the blackberries are ready, and the birds are so fond of them that they greedily eat the fruits as soon as they begin to ripen. Mulberries were one of the favorite fruits of the Indians, but they always had a race with their feathered neighbors when it came time to gather them.

Mulberries are so perishable that it would be impossible to sell them in the markets, but they are one of the most delicious of the wild fruits. They are fine to eat just as they come from the tree, for they are so sweet that they need no sugar. Country boys today enjoy them every bit as much as the Indians did. And their mothers know, too, that they make excellent pies, jellies, and preserves. One can dry them also and keep some for winter use—just as the Indians did long ago.

Fruit

Leaf

Red Mulberry

The Olax Family

TALLOWWOOD (*Ximenia americana*)

In his famous book, *Travels Through North &
South Carolina, Georgia, East & West Florida,*
the eighteenth century Quaker naturalist
William Bartram mentioned a tree called the
"wild lime" or the "tallownut." *Today* it is more
commonly known as the tallowwood or the hog
plum. In the scrubs of central Florida it grows
as a low spiny shrub; but in the hammocks it
often becomes a small tree.

One could very easily mistake the tallowwood
for some kind of citrus. It produces fragrant
flowers and both green and ripened fruits
throughout the year, and it has quite citruslike
evergreen leaves. Its soft, yellow, plumlike fruits
were described by Bartram has having "the con-
stance, looks & tastes like a custard having a little
tartness."

According to Bartram, the fruits of the tallowwood were highly esteemed by the Florida
Indians. They apparently have much less appeal
to modern palates, for not many people today
recommend them very highly.

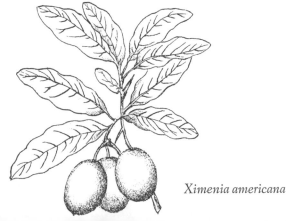

Ximenia americana

COMMON POKE, OR POKEWEED
(*Phytolacca americana*)

Many people still enjoy the tender young shoots of the common poke, or pokeweed, as much as the Indians did long ago. In the South "poke salad" is a very popular spring green. The young shoots must be cut when they are no more than about six inches high. They may be eaten simply as boiled greens or prepared in the same ways as asparagus. After being cooked in a change or two of water, the poke shoots are quite wholesome and have a very pleasant taste.

In gathering poke, one must be careful not to include any of the root of the plant as it contains a poison. It is best to snap or cut the shoots off an inch or so above the ground. Later in the year the tall, branching poke plants are a familiar sight in old fields, woods borders, and along the country roadsides. Although the drooping clusters of shiny black berries look quite tempting in the summer and fall, they should *not* be eaten. Some people call them "ink berries," and they are indeed full of a deep purple juice. Many birds and wild mammals feast on them without harm, but unfortunately they have been known to poison children.

Pokeweed Phytolacca americana

The Purslane Family

SPRING BEAUTIES (*Claytonia*)

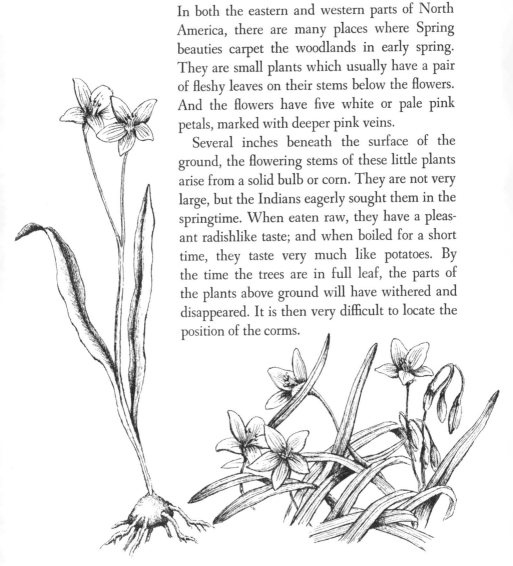

In both the eastern and western parts of North America, there are many places where Spring beauties carpet the woodlands in early spring. They are small plants which usually have a pair of fleshy leaves on their stems below the flowers. And the flowers have five white or pale pink petals, marked with deeper pink veins.

Several inches beneath the surface of the ground, the flowering stems of these little plants arise from a solid bulb or corn. They are not very large, but the Indians eagerly sought them in the springtime. When eaten raw, they have a pleasant radishlike taste; and when boiled for a short time, they taste very much like potatoes. By the time the trees are in full leaf, the parts of the plants above ground will have withered and disappeared. It is then very difficult to locate the position of the corms.

Claytonia virginica

BITTERROOT (*Lewisia rediviva*)

The bitterroot is a stemless little plant with a tuft of fleshy and narrow leaves an inch or two long. It grows from Montana and Colorado westward. Beneath the ground, it has a carrot-shaped and starchy root which was an important food of the Indians and the early settlers. The roots were dug in the early spring for at this time they are tender and most nutritive. By late spring, too, the leaves wither and disappear; but they are followed by pretty, many-petaled, white to pinkish flowers an inch or two across.

Roots of the bitterroot are indeed intensely bitter when raw, but the bitterness largely disappears when they are cooked. The outer covering of the roots slips off easily, leaving a fleshy white core; this the Indians baked, or boiled, or ground into meal.

The name *Lewisia* honors Captain Meriwether Lewis, for it was one of the western plants collected during the famous Lewis and Clark Expedition. Quite likely, the members of that expedition used the starchy roots as food.

The bitterroot is the State Flower of Montana.

Bitterroot

The Water-Lily Family

AMERICAN NELUMBO (*Nelumbo lutea*)

During the summer the American nelumbo, which is also known as the yellow lotus and the water chinquapin, has beautiful pale yellow flowers from six to ten inches across. They are followed by children's top-shaped structures which have seedlike fruits sunk in pits on their upper surface. The seeds look very much like small acorns, and they are both tasty and nutritious. The Indians consumed them raw, boiled them, and roasted them in hot coals. Sometimes they were parched, to loosen the kernels from the hard outer shells, and then ground into meal. This meal was used in making bread or often boiled with meat to make soup.

Deep down in the muck, the nelumbo has a very long rootstock that is full of starch between autumn and late spring. The Indians prized the roots as much as they did the seedlike fruits, and they ate them either boiled or baked. In early summer they also enjoyed the tender young leaves, which were used as boiled greens. It is easy to see why the nelumbo was such a great favorite of the Indians. Some botanists believe that the Indians brought the nelumbo from the Mississippi Valley and planted it in many of the eastern waters where it is still found today.

Flower

Leaf

Fruit

Nelumbo lutea

Fruit

Flower

eaf

phar advena

Indians Gathering Yellow Water Lily Fruits

FOODS FROM OTHER WATER LILIES

Other members of the water-lily family also provided the Indians with food. They often waded into the beds of the tuberous water lily (*Nymphaea tuberosa*), breaking off its edible starch-filled tubers. The yellow-flowered pond lilies or spatterdocks (*Nuphar*) have large seeds which they often gathered and roasted. The roasted seeds, which the Klamath Indians called "wokas," are said to have a taste quite similar to that of popcorn. Pond lilies also have big snakelike rootstocks which creep through the muck. Sometimes, when they were hard-pressed for food, the Indians boiled or baked them.

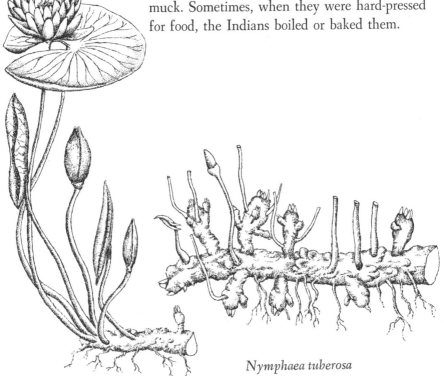

Nymphaea tuberosa

MARSH MARIGOLD (*Caltha palustris*)

Early in the spring, wet places from the shores of the North Atlantic west as far as Alaska, and southward into Virginia and Nebraska, are filled with the bright golden-yellow blossoms of marsh marigolds. Their big blooms resemble buttercups and make a pretty sight. But the shiny roundish leaves with scalloped edges were an even more beautiful sight to the Indians hungry for spring greens.

The early settlers soon discovered two things. The first was that the marsh marigold was not as poisonous as people in the Old World had long supposed it to be, and secondly, that the young leaves made delicious boiled greens. In fact, they liked them so much that marsh marigolds have been a popular spring green ever since, and to this day one can buy them in spring in the markets of New England. New Englanders, and Pennsylvanians, too, have always preferred to call them "cowslip greens."

Marsh Marigold

The Barberry Family

MAYAPPLE (*Podophyllum peltatum*)

Each spring patches of mayapple plants push their way above ground and open their umbrella-like leaves in woodlands throughout the eastern United States. The young plants have but a solitary leaf that looks like a shield. Older ones have a stem which forks, and in the crotch formed by the pair of leaves hangs a large, waxy, white blossom with golden-yellow stamens. Later in the summer, the blossom is replaced by a big berry which, both in shape and color, reminds one of a lemon.

Most boys, like the Indians of yesteryear, seem to be quite fond of the ripened mayapple fruits. Grownups, as a rule, are much less enthusiastic about them. The fruits have a peculiar flavor—quite unlike that of any familiar fruit—and many regard them as being sickeningly sweet. When fully ripe, however, they are perfectly edible, although other parts of the plant are poisonous. Rootstocks of the mayapple are used medicinally.

Fruit

Leaves

Flower

Mayapple

The Custard-Apple Family

COMMON PAPAW (*Asimina triloba*)

The common papaw is a small tree with such a tropical appearance that it seems out of place in our woodlands. And well it might seem so, for it belongs to a family of mostly tropical plants. It is often common along the streams and in low woods from the Mississippi Valley eastward to the Atlantic Coast. Every country boy within its range is familiar with its fruits, which look very much like stubby bananas.

Papaws are at their best in the fall, after the skins have turned blackish and become wrinkled. Then the pulp within the better ones becomes golden-yellow, soft, and sweet and spicy. No one has described them better than the poet James Whitcomb Riley, who likened a ripened papaw to a "custard pie without a crust." And needless to say, the Indians never failed to harvest this delicious fruit.

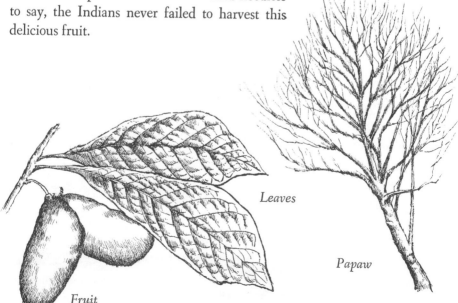

Leaves

Papaw

Fruit

TOOTHWORTS (*Dentaria*)

In the woodlands of eastern North America, the toothworts are usually among the commonest and most familiar of spring wildflowers. Their flowers have four white or purple-tinged petals. As in the flowers of all other members of the mustard family, they are always arranged in the form of a cross.

The cut-leaf toothwort (*Dentaria laciniata*) usually has three leaves arranged in a circle about the stem, and they are deeply cut or divided. Beneath the ground, it has little tubers shaped very much like tiny sweet potatoes.

Another common relative, the two-leaf toothwort (*Dentaria diphylla*), has a pair of stem leaves which are divided into three egg-shaped leaflets with toothed edges. Underground, it has a long and wrinkled rootstock from which it often gets the name of "crinkleroot."

The tubers or rootstocks of all the toothworts are white, crisp, and have a mildly peppery taste. Undoubtedly, the Indians often dug them up and ate them, although it would require a good many to make a meal. Like many boys and girls today, they probably used them as a pleasant nibble while on treks through the forest.

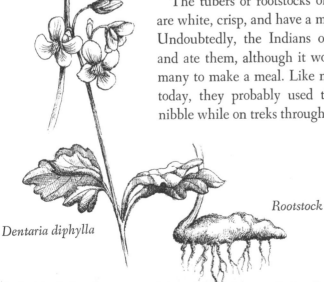

Dentaria laciniata

Dentaria diphylla

Rootstock

The Saxifrage Family

CURRANTS AND GOOSEBERRIES
(*Ribes*)

Currants and gooseberries were among the sum-
mertime fruits the Indians harvested. A number
of species of them are found in various parts of
North America. All of them have edible fruits,
but some are quite tart—almost too sour to be
eaten raw. Pioneer housewives, however, found
very good uses for the fruits in excellent pies,
jellies, and preserves. In western Montana,
Lewis and Clark feasted on purple, yellow, and
black currants, which were "more pleasing to
the palate than those grown in their Virginia
home gardens."

Gooseberries

The Indians did not use the fruits to make
jellies or pies, but they usually dried plenty of
currants for winter use. They often added them
to their pemmican, a food made from dried
buffalo meat and fat pounded together and
formed into the shape of loaves or cakes. Indian
hunters and warriors carried this concentrated
food with them on long journeys.

Unfortunately currants and gooseberries are
alternate hosts of a rust fungus which attacks
the white or five-needled pines. The fungus cannot spread from pine to pine. It must complete

a stage of its life cycle on the leaves of currant or gooseberry bushes. Spores produced on the leaves of these bushes are then able to infect pines. So foresters try to eliminate currants and gooseberries from the places where white pines are important timber trees.

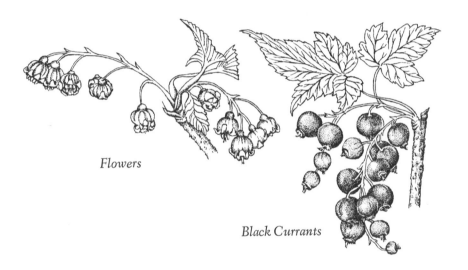

Flowers

Black Currants

Blackfeet Indians
Four stages of Preparing Pemmican

The Rose Family

ROSES (*Rosa*)

Many species of wild roses are found in North America, and their beautiful flowers are followed by peculiar "fruits" which are called hips. Rose hips are not really fruits. They are the swollen and fleshy tips of the flower stalks, and inside of them are the real fruits. Many of us mistake these for seeds.

Rose hips often remain on the bushes throughout the winter. Thus they frequently provided the Indians with a taste of fresh fruit during the "lean and hungry" season of the year. Rose hips are quite edible, and the early settlers likewise used them as food. They have long been used as food by peoples in the northern parts of Europe and Asia.

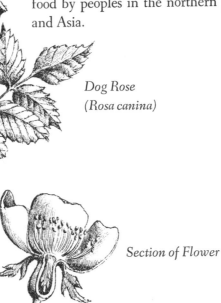

Dog Rose
(*Rosa canina*)

Section of Flower

WILD STRAWBERRIES (*Fragaria*)

To many of the Indians, our month of June was the "Strawberry Moon." The wild strawberries were always among the first of the wild fruits to ripen. In most places the ripening took place in June, but in the Southeast the berries usually ripened nearly a month earlier. Northward, and in the higher mountains, the strawberries often were not ripe until well into the summer.

Several species and varieties of wild strawberries are found in the New World. The plants grew abundantly in the natural meadows and open woodlands, and the Indian women and children gathered the fruits in large quantities. Everybody was fond of the bright red, fragrant, sweet, and juicy fruits. Wild strawberries are smaller than the cultivated ones we have today, but they are usually far sweeter. They have a flavor that no cultivated strawberry can quite match.

Strawberries were no strangers to the early settlers. They had long been familiar with the ones which grew in the Old World. But they were amazed at the vigor of the New World plants and the abundance of fine fruits they pro-

Flower

Strawberry

Fruit

duced. Thus, early in the seventeenth century, the common wild strawberry (*Fragaria virginiana*) of eastern North America was being grown in European gardens. Some time afterward the sand strawberry (*Fragaria chiloensis*) of the Pacific Coast was likewise introduced into Europe. In the gardens of the Old World, these two New World strawberries were crossed. From these and later crosses came the various varieties of cultivated strawberries.

Strawberries are no more fruits than rose hips are, and neither are they berries. The real strawberry fruits are those "seeds" on the surface of the strawberry, while the main part of the strawberry develops from the tip of the stalk to which the parts of the blossom are attached.

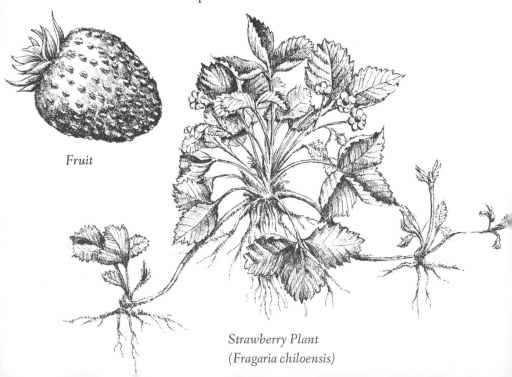

Fruit

Strawberry Plant
(*Fragaria chiloensis*)

BLACKBERRIES AND RASPBERRIES
(Rubus)

Blackberries and raspberries were as familiar to the Indians as they are to us today. Many kinds of blackberries, as well as both the red-fruited and black-fruited raspberries, have always grown in America. After the settlers cleared the land, the berries grew even more abundantly. They form the familiar brier patches in abandoned fields and along roadsides and fences. Every summer a great many people go forth, pail in hand, to pick the wild fruits. Our cultivated blackberries have all been developed from the wild American plants, and so have the cultivated black raspberries. Some of the garden red raspberries were derived by crossing native plants with the European red raspberry.

Blackberry

The "fruits" of blackberries and raspberries are actually clusters of miniature stone fruits, like small cherries. When one picks blackberries, or the trailing dewberries, the tip of the flower stalk comes off with the cluster of fruits. In raspberries, however, we pull the cluster of little fruits off the flower stalk, leaving a hollow inside the berry. For this reason many people call the raspberries "thimbleberries."

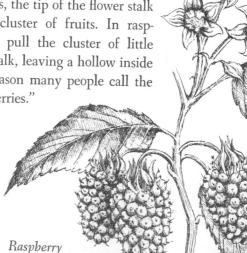

Raspberry

SHADBUSHES, OR JUNEBERRIES
(*Amelanchier*)

Each spring, about the time the shad are running up the streams from the ocean, the shad-
bushes whiten the valley and hillsides with their
blooms. A number of species of them grow in
various parts of North America. Some are small
trees. Some are tall shrubs; others are low woody
plants. In bloom, they are so beautiful that they
are sometimes grown as ornamental plants. In
various places they are known as Juneberries,
serviceberries, and sarviceberries.

The fruits are not really berries. They are very
much like tiny apples and they vary from dark
blue to purplish-black when fully ripe. Some are
rather dry and tasteless, but the best of them are
sweet, juicy, and pleasant tasting. Few people
today enjoy these wild fruits, but both the
Indians and the early settlers always made good
use of them. They are delicious eaten raw; in
earlier days they were often cooked as a sauce
and used in pies.

The Indians not only ate the fresh raw fruits
but preserved quantities of them for use during
the winter. Quite often they were mashed into
a pasty pulp and then dried in the form of cakes
to be used for winter puddings. The dried fruits
were also mixed with meat and fat to make
pemmican.

Shadbush

WILD CRAB APPLES (*Malus*)

The Indians had no big and delicious apples such as we have today, but there have always been apples in America. In the springtime the spiny little apple trees always scented the air with the strong fragrance of their pink blossoms. In the fall they have always borne crops of small greenish-yellow apples. They have a greasy feel when they are handled and they are delightfully fragrant, but they are as hard as rocks and intensely sour. We know them as wild crab apples.

Both the Indians and the early settlers made very good use of the wild crab apples. They frequently gathered quantities of them in the late fall and buried them in pits dug in the ground. By late winter or early spring the ones which did not rot became a bit more mellow and lost some of their intense sourness. They were quite good when boiled with maple syrup or sugar. Some country people still use them for making jellies. Pure wild crab-apple jelly has a clear orange-red color and a most pleasant tart flavor.

Fruit

Wild Crab Apple

Flower

84

Flower

Fruit

Hawthorn

HAWTHORNS (*Crataegus*)

The Indians also enjoyed the fruits of the hawthorns, which boys usually call just "haws." In spring the thorny little trees or bushes are almost covered with white blossoms. Almost every fall they are usually laden with small applelike fruits. Often they are a beautiful bright red, but some species have fruits which are yellow, purplish, or even nearly black in color. The Indians frequently ate the raw fruits, but they also cooked them with maple sugar. They also dried them for mixing in their pemmican. Even today some of the country people use the fruits for making jelly, but large quantities of them go to waste every fall.

WILD PLUMS AND CHERRIES (*Prunus*)

Several kinds of wild plums grow in various parts of North America, and the Indians always harvested their fruits. The early settlers found many thickets of the Chickasaw plum (*Prunus angustifolia*) in the Southeast. These little trees or bushes bore excellent plums that ripened in June or early July, and the red or yellow fruits

Flower

Chickasaw Plum
(*Prunus angustifolia*)

Fruit

were sweet and delicious. The Indians prized
this plum most highly. They claimed that it had
come from beyond the "Great River," which we
call the Mississippi. No doubt many, if not most,
of the plum thickets were intentionally planted
by the Indians. Like a few of the other native
plums, it became a parent of some of our cultivated varieties.

Several species of cherries grew in America,
too. None of them bore fruits nearly as good as
the cultivated cherries we have today, but they
were always used by the Indians.

The fruits of the black cherry (*Prunus serotina*), when fully ripe in late summer or early
fall, have quite a delightful bitter-sweet and
winy taste. They can be eaten raw with pleasure.
Those of the fire or pin cherry (*Prunus pennsylvanica*), which are bright red and look like
miniatures of our familiar pie cherries, are as
intensely sour as the native crab apples. The
deep red to blackish fruits of the chokecherry
(*Prunus virginiana*) look tempting, too, but they
are bound to pucker one's mouth. Still many of
the Indians seem to have enjoyed them, and they
usually dried them for winter use. Many people
use the fruits of wild cherries for making jelly,
mixing the cherry juice with that of apples or
crab apples.

Prunus serotina

*Prunus
pennsylvanica*

Prunus virginiana

The Pea Family

INDIAN BREADROOT (*Psoralea esculenta*)

The Indian breadroot was one of the most important food plants of the plains Indians. It has a large turnip-shaped root that is full of starch, and the Indians regularly harvested quantities of them during the early summer. Sometimes they simply peeled them and ate them raw, for they enjoyed the sweetish, turniplike taste. They also boiled or roasted them, just as we do potatoes. Slices of the peeled roots were strung on strings and dried in the sun for winter use, for in winter they ground them into meal or cooked them with meat.

Our early explorers, trappers, and the settlers who followed them found that the roots were delicious, as well as very nutritious. It was not long before the plant became known by a variety of names other than breadroot. Those who spoke English called it the prairie-turnip, prairie-apple, or prairie-potato. Among the French-speaking traders and trappers it became known as the *pomme blanche* and *pomme de prairie*.

Unlike the Indians who dwelt in the eastern forests or those living in the Southwest, the plains Indians seldom if ever grew crops such as corn, squashes, and beans. For the most part, they were hunters, and they followed the great herds of bison which once roamed the West. These Indians depended almost entirely upon wild food plants, such as the breadroot, for their vegetable food.

(Before the horse came)
Kiowa Buffalo Hunters Follow the
Herds

Root

Psoralea
esculenta

GROUNDNUT, OR WILD BEAN
(Apios americana)

One should look for the groundnut, or wild
bean, in low grounds, along streams or about
the borders of swamps and marshes. It is a
slender twining vine, and in summer it has little
clusters of chocolate-brown, beanlike blossoms.
They are followed by little pods which resemble
beans.

Beneath the surface of the ground, the plant
has edible tubers which the eastern Indians
prized as highly as the plains Indians did the
breadroot. Sometimes they are as big as small
hens' eggs, and usually several of them grow together along the stringy roots. Few of the native
food plants attracted the attention of the early
colonists as much as the groundnut, which they
frequently called the "Indian-potato." They, too,
found the starchy tubers to be both nourishing
and savory, especially after being baked or
boiled. It is said that the Pilgrims practically
lived on groundnut tubers during their first
winter in the New World.

Apios americana

HOG PEANUT, OR WILD PEANUT
(Amphicarpa bracteata)

The hog, or wild, peanut is another twining
vine that grows in moist woods and thickets in
the East. During the summer, it has small
clusters of little white or pale purple flowers in
the axils of its three-parted leaves. These flowers
develop into little pods about an inch long,
resembling bean pods, but near the base of the
plant there are flowers of another kind. They are
barely noticeable for they have no showy petals,
and they grow on threadlike runners. These
flowers later develop into roundish pods, containing a single large seed. And like those of the
true peanut, the seeds develop beneath the
ground.

Many of the Indians used the wild peanut
seeds as food. Field mice are fond of them, too,
and the little rodents often store as many as
several quarts of them in their nests. Quite often
the Indians obtained their supply by raiding the
stores of the little animals. The Dakotas, however, seem to have had a custom of leaving an
equal amount of corn or other food in exchange.

Amphicarpa bracteata

MESQUITES (*Prosopis*) and
PALOVERDES (*Cercidium*)

The thorny mesquite trees have beanlike pods which are a choice food of the Indians living in the dry Southwest. They are often called "honey-pods" because of the sweet pulp that surrounds the seeds. The Indians cook the green pods the way we do snap beans, and they also grind the dried seeds into meal for baking a very nutritious bread.

Paloverdes, which also grow in the arid Southwest, are quite showy little trees when they are covered with bright yellow blossoms in the early spring. The blooms are followed later by beanlike pods, which the Indians use in the same ways as those of the mesquites.

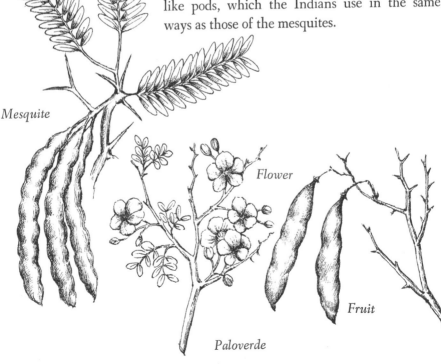

Mesquite

Flower

Fruit

Paloverde

SUMACS (*Rhus*)

Wherever red-fruited sumacs grew, their fruits were gathered by the Indians. To look at them one would wonder why, for there seems to be nothing at all about them that anyone could eat. Even the birds pass them up, and the fruits usually remain on the trees or bushes all through the winter. They are indeed a food of last resort.

Sumac fruits look like berries, but they consist largely of a hard stone which contains a seed. They look fuzzy because they are covered by a thin skin with a great many tiny red hairs. These hairs, however, contain an acid, and from the sumac fruits the Indians made a pleasantly sour drink—in both looks and taste very much like pink lemonade. The Indians were so fond of it that they often stored the fruits so they could enjoy the drink during the winter.

To make this "Indian lemonade," the fruits should be gathered in summer or early fall, and of course care should be taken to avoid the clusters which are too worm-eaten. After soaking the bruised fruits in cold water for several hours, the liquid should be strained through a cloth to remove the hairs, though it is doubtful that the Indians went to the trouble of doing this. You

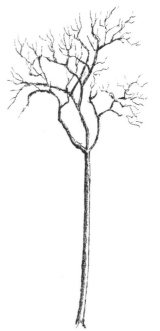

Sumac

will no doubt want to add some sugar, as you would to real lemonade, before drinking it. Lots of people have enjoyed this "Indian lemonade" just as much as the Indians did. More than likely you would, too.

*Staghorn
Sumac*

Leaves

Fruit

The Maple Family

SUGAR MAPLE (*Acer saccharum*)

The Indians obtained sugar from the sap of
several kinds of trees; from the maples, birches,
hickories, and even butternut trees. But that of
one kind of maple was always preferred, and
wherever it grew, the Indians always chose it
above all the other trees. Its sap is sweeter than
that of most other trees, even that of the other
kinds of maples. It was from its sweet sap that
the sugar maple got its name.

Quite likely the Indians discovered the sweet-
ness of the sap by some mere accident. Out of
curiosity, one of them may have tasted the
watery liquid flowing from the rows of holes
which sapsuckers had drilled in the trunk of a
tree. He had noticed that it always attracted the
mourning-cloak butterflies when they came out
of their winter hiding places during the first
warm sunny days. When he tasted it, he found
that it was sweet; and in time the Indians
learned how to obtain sugar from the sweet sap.

There is an old Menominee legend which ex-
plains why the Indians had to work so hard to
obtain the sugar. One day old grandmother,
Nokomis, showed Manabusha, the great friend
of mankind, how to tap the trees and obtain the

Sugar Maple

Northeastern Indians
Preparing Maple Syrup

sap. When she made a gash in the trunk of the maple tree, a thick syrupy sap flowed out, which quickly hardened into sugar. The wise Manabusha realized that this was very bad, for people would not work if they could obtain the sugar so easily and they would become lazy. So he climbed to the top of the tallest tree, and with his hand he sprinkled water over the trees like rain. Ever afterward a watery sap flowed from the trees. The Indians now had to make bark troughs in which to gather the sap. They had to gather a lot of firewood, too, for the sap had to boil day and night before it became thick enough to harden into sugar.

There was always great activity in the forest while the maple sap was flowing, for the time of sugar-making ended when the buds began to swell. With stone axes they made deep gashes through the bark of the trees. Then hollow reeds or wooden spouts were placed beneath the gashes, so the sap would drip into small troughs made of bark or animal skins. Sap from these little troughs was emptied into a big trough, which was usually a hollowed-out log.

Before the Europeans came to America, the Indians had no metal kettles in which the sap could be boiled. Stones constantly had to be heated and put into the big trough to keep the sap boiling. As it boiled, it became thicker and thicker. At last it became thick enough to harden into sugar when it cooled. Then it was poured into molds so the sap would harden into small cakes of sugar.

The Indians were very fond of maple sugar. Indian children enjoyed nibbling on the sugar cakes like candy. At sugar-making time, some of the thick hot syrup was poured over popped corn and rolled into balls, always a very special treat. Warriors and hunters always carried with them the nourishing food they called pemmican. The northeastern Indians usually made it by mixing maple sugar with dried venison or bear meat, and often some dried berries.

The first explorers and the early settlers were amazed when they learned that the Indians obtained a fine sugar from the sap of trees. Nobody in the civilized countries of the Old World had ever thought of such a thing, and even the learned scientists of that day hailed it as a remarkable discovery. The early settlers, however, soon learned how to make the syrup and sugar; and eventually great improvements were made in the process.

In pioneer days, and for a long time thereafter,

maple sugar was a staple food. It was the only
kind of sugar to be had. But after cane sugar
became so easy to obtain in the stores,
the use of maple sugar quickly declined.
Quite a lot of maple syrup is still produced today
from New England westward to the Great Lakes
region, and southward into the mountains of
West Virginia. Pure maple syrup is so expensive
today that we think of it as a luxury. It is one of
the most popular of the foods that have been
handed down to us from the Indians.

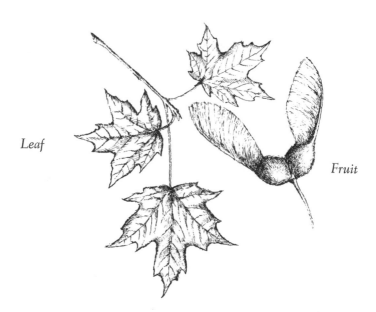

Leaf

Fruit

The Vine Family

WILD GRAPES (*Vitis*)

A number of different kinds of wild grapes grow profusely in various parts of North America, and their fruits were always gathered by the Indians. The Vikings, who were the first Europeans to visit the New World, found such an abundance of grape vines along the northeastern coast that they gave it the name of Vinland.

Most of the wild grapes, however, were a disappointment to the early settlers. They were much inferior to the fine table and wine grapes they had known in the Old World. The fruits of the majority of American grapes were quite small, and they were very seedy and intensely sour. Some of them improved a bit after the fall frosts, but they were regarded as fit only for making jelly.

Many attempts were made by the colonists to grow the European grapes, but they always met with failure. However, among the New World

Vitis labrusca

grapes there were two that held some promise. One of these was the fox grape (*Vitis labrusca*), which still grows along streams and in low woodlands from Maine westward to Michigan and southward to the Gulf of Mexico. It bears fairly large fruits which are purplish-black to brownish-purple or, rarely, amber in color; and they have a pleasantly sweet and musky flavor. The fox grape became the parent of the Concord and the other cultivated grapes that are used extensively for grape juice, jelly, and jam.

In the Southeast grew another wild grape which was a great favorite of the Indians. This was the muscadine (*Vitis rotundifolia*). It bore fruits sometimes almost an inch in diameter, purplish-black to bronze in color, with a very tough skin, but with a very sweet and musky taste. The wild muscadine was soon brought into cultivation and became the parent of the scuppernongs, the most popular of grapes in the South.

Vitis rotundifolia

The Passionflower Family

MAYPOPS (*Passiflora incarnata*)

In the Southeast there is a trailing or somewhat climbing vine, usually with three-lobed leaves. It has attractive, oddly fringed, big white and lavender flowers. It often grows abundantly along the roadsides and in fields and thickets. Although it is one of the plants universally known as passionflowers, in the South it is familiar to all as the maypop.

Maypop fruits are well known to most southern children. They are big berries, and true ones, about the size and shape of hens' eggs; when fully ripe, they become a light green or yellowish in color. Children, and even some grownups, enjoy the taste of the sweet but mildly acid fruits. Others say that they are more edible than enjoyable. The Indians seem to have thought well of them, and according to Captain John Smith, the Virginia Indians often cultivated the plants for their fruits.

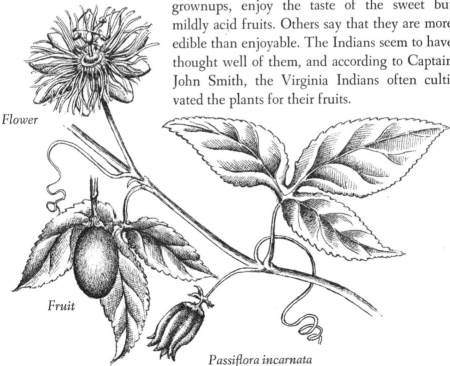

Flower

Fruit

Passiflora incarnata

The Papaya Family

PAPAYA (*Carica papaya*)

The papaya is a native of tropical America, but
it has been so widely cultivated that its original
home is unknown. It is a soft-stemmed, treelike
plant that produces delicious fruits very similar
to melons, and it is well known throughout
southern Florida and other tropical lands. Papaya
fruits have a milky juice which contains papain
—a substance used medicinally to aid digestion,
and also used in making the meat tenderizers
that are sold in the grocery stores.

In many places in southern Florida, the
papaya grows in a wild state, but how it got to
Florida is somewhat of a mystery. It may have
been brought there by Indians a very long time
ago, or it may have been introduced by some
of the early Spanish explorers. At any rate, it
must have grown farther north than it does
today, for William Bartram saw the plants along
the upper St. John's River during his visit to
Florida in the 1770's. The Florida Indians seem
to have enjoyed papaya fruits as much as Flor-
idians do today.

Carica papaya

Fruit

The Cactus Family

PRICKLY PEARS, OR INDIAN FIGS
(*Opuntia*)

Some of the prickly-pear cacti grow in Florida and other eastern states, but we know little, if anything, about the usage of their fruits by the eastern Indians. In the arid Southwest, however, the Indians have always gathered quantities of them and they are popularly known as "Indian figs."

The showy blossoms, and the fruits which follow them, grow along the edges of the flattened green joints that make up the cactus stems. They are usually low enough so that the fruits can be picked by hand, but first the tufts of tiny bristly spines must be removed. The Indian women deftly dust them off with brushes made from branches of the creosote bush, and quickly fill their baskets with the fruits.

Prickly-pear fruits are sweet and juicy. They are said to be excellent thirst-quenchers, and the Indians enjoy them both raw and cooked. The parched seeds are used as a thickening for soup. Sometimes even the younger joints of the plants are boiled or roasted and used as food.

Opuntia picus-indica

Opuntia compressa

SAGUARO, OR GIANT CACTUS
(Cereus giganteus)

The Papago and the Pima Indians of Arizona still harvest the fruits of the saguaro (pronounced either sah-*gwha*-ro or sah-*wha*-ro), just as their ancestors did a long time ago. Each year, during the month of July, the Indian families camp out in the groves of the giant cacti. They are there to gather the fruits, which grow in clusters atop the tall stems and armlike branches of the saguaros. This is the time of the year when the fruits ripen. And as they ripen, they usually split open, exposing the bright scarlet and sugary pulp that is mixed with tiny black seeds.

To reach the fruits on their lofty perches, Indian women use long poles made from the sturdy wooden ribs of other saguaros—saguaros that have died. They carefully select the ripe fruits from among the green ones and bring them down to the ground. Other women and children pick up the fallen fruits and put them into brightly colored baskets. When the baskets are full, the women carry them back to camp, usually balancing them on their heads.

In the camp, other women are busy cooking the fruits and straining them through a big

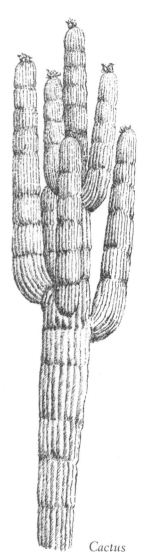

Cactus

*Pima Indians Gathering
Saguaro Cactus Fruits*

loosely woven basket. The basket allows the juice to pass through it into a large pot beneath; then it is slowly boiled until it becomes a syrup. The pulpy part of the fruit, which remains in the basket, is not wasted. It is spread out to dry in the hot desert sun after most of the seeds have been removed. The dried pulp is used for making preserves and wine. Some of it is also stored for winter use.

Flower and Fruit

The Carrot Family

The carrot family contains some of the finest edible plants, but also some deadly poisonous ones. No members of the family should be used as food until the correct identification is *certain*. Some of the plants, though quite similar in appearance to edible species, are extremely poisonous.

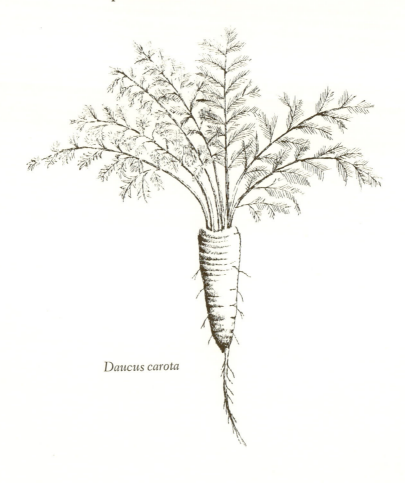

Daucus carota

YAMPA, OR SQUAWROOT (*Perideridia gairdneri*)

Yampa, or squawroot, is a very close relative of the caraway—a plant often grown in herb gardens. In summer, it has flat-topped clusters of small white flowers. They look quite like the flowers of the familiar wayside weed which we call the wild carrot or Queen Anne's lace, but the clusters are more open. It grows from one to three feet tall, with a slender stem along which are leaves divided into narrow and grasslike leaflets.

The Indians dug the fleshy roots of the yampa in spring and early summer. They often cooked them with meat, but they also dried them and ground them into meal or flour. By many, yampa roots have been rated as the finest of all the Indian foods of western America. Lewis and Clark used them during their expedition, and many other explorers seem to have enjoyed them as much as the Indian did. They can be used in the same ways as parsnips or potatoes, and when cooked they are sweet and mealy.

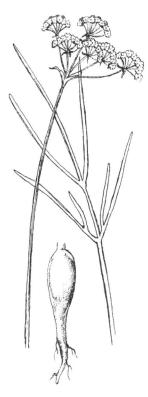

Yampa

BISCUITROOTS (*Lomatium*)

Several species of the biscuitroot grow in the West. They are all rather low plants, with flat-topped clusters of small yellow or white flowers similar to those of the yampa. The fleshy roots of the biscuitroots were another important food of the western Indians. Along with those of the yampa, they were among their chief articles of trade. In the journals of their expedition, Lewis and Clark mention trading buttons, beads, and various other trinkets to the Indians for a supply of "cows."

"Cous" or "cowas" were Indian names for the biscuitroots, but to the white men the name sounded very much like "cows." Thus it was biscuitroots, not cattle, that the famous explorers were referring to.

After the roots were peeled and dried, the Indians ground them into flour which was used to make flat cakes. Sometimes the cakes were so large that they were simply strapped on a saddle if they were to be carried on long journeys. Although the cakes were wholesome and nutritious, to the white men they tasted so much like stale biscuits that they gave the plants the name of biscuitroots.

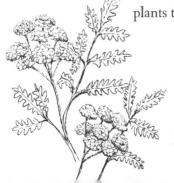

Bisquitroot

COW PARSNIP (*Heracleum lanatum*)

From Newfoundland to Alaska, and south in the mountains to North Carolina and Colorado, the cow parsnip is a familiar plant. It is a big plant, often five feet of more tall, with large three-parted leaves and a flat-topped cluster of small white flowers—this cluster sometimes being as much as a foot across. The Indians, and even the Eskimos, know the cow parsnip well. In spring, the young stems are peeled and eaten either raw or cooked, and sometimes the roots are also eaten as a cooked vegetable.

Among the Blackfeet, the cow parsnip is regarded as a sacred plant, and stalks of it are placed upon an altar during their sun dances and other ceremonials.

Leaf

Root

Plant

Cow Parsnip

The Heath Family

BLUEBERRIES (*Vaccinium*) and HUCKLEBERRIES (*Gaylussacia*)

Many kinds of wild blueberries and huckleberries provided the Indians with delicious fruit, and they are still eagerly sought by berry pickers. Some kinds of blueberries grew on tall bushes in the swamps, while others grew on lower bushes in the uplands. They were extremely abundant in the places where fires had swept through the forests, and there had always been fires in the forests of primitive America. Many of the fires were caused by lightning. Others were caused by the Indians themselves. The great pine forests owed their existence to the periodic fires. Otherwise the land would have been occupied by forests of hardwood trees—such as oaks, ashes, beeches, birches, and maples.

Blueberries have often, but quite incorrectly, been called "huckleberries." The bushes of both produce edible fruit. But the true huckleberries have fruits containing but ten fairly large seeds, and at least the lower surfaces of their leaves are covered with minute specks of yellowish resin. Blueberries, on the other hand, have many very small seeds; their leaves never

Gaylussacia baccata
Black Huckleberry

have any resin dots. The Indian berry pickers, like berry pickers today, made little or no distinction between them. Some kinds of blueberries and huckleberries have fruits which are better than others; but the best of them are sweet, and spicy, and juicy.

Some varieties of blueberries have been tamed and are now grown commercially. They bear fruits which are much larger than those of the wild plants; but like cultivated strawberries, they somehow lack the delicious spicy flavor of the wild fruits. In Maine, the Pocono Mountains of Pennsylvania, and other places, too, the wild blueberries are still gathered in great quantities for the market. And for obvious reasons, the makers of muffin and pancake mixes are careful to point out that their products contain *wild* blueberries.

The Indians always dried great quantities of the fruits in the sun so that in winter they could use them in their puddings, cakes, and pemmican. Country people have always canned them for use in pies and muffins during the winter. They also make preserves and excellent jelly from the juice of blueberries mixed with that of apples or wild crab apples.

Flower

Vacciium Corymbosum
Highbush Blueberry

Indian Women Gathering
Cranberries in a Bog

Flower

Fruit

AMERICAN CRANBERRY (*Vaccinium macrocarpum*)

Every one of us is familiar with the cranberries sold in the stores during the late fall, and with the cranberry sauce that is served along with the Thanksgiving turkey. What a perfect combination of Indian foods it is, as both turkeys and cranberries are gifts of the New World. It is not at all unlikely that the Indians contributed both to the Pilgrims' first Thanksgiving dinner.

The American cranberry is a low trailing vine which grows in boggy places from New England westward to the Great Lakes Region, and locally southward to the coast and mountains of North Carolina.

Every fall, usually after the bogs froze hard enough to support their weight, the Indians went into them to harvest the red berries. Like the wild crab apples, they are much too tart to be eaten raw, but the Indians enjoyed them when they were cooked with maple sugar. The berries keep well, and hence they had fresh fruits to eat during a large part of the winter.

The cranberries we buy in the stores today are grown in carefully flooded bogs. Fresh berries arrive on the market in time for Thanksgiving and are usually available until the Christmas season, but canned cranberry sauce and cranberry juice are on the grocer's shelves all year round.

PERSIMMON (*Diospyros virginiana*)

Persimmons are familiar wild fruits throughout the Southeast, where the trees grow abundantly in the pinelands and old fields from the coast to the lower mountains.

Persimmons are fruits of the fall season. As a rule, they are not fully ripe and at their best until hard frosts have occurred. Then the best of them become soft as mush, but sweet and most pleasant in taste. However, as Captain John Smith wrote in his diary, "If it be not ripe, it will draw a man's mouth awrie with much torment." It is difficult to imagine anything that will pucker the mouth more than an unripe persimmon.

Indians of the Southeast harvested the persimmon fruits in large quantities, and they often dried them for winter use. It was from the Indians that the early settlers learned how to make persimmon pudding and persimmon bread.

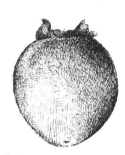

Fruit

Diospyros virginiana

MILKWEED (*Asclepias*)

The tender young shoots of milkweeds were used by the Indians as greens, and are so used by many other people in recent times. Like poke shoots, they must be cut when just a few inches tall. They cannot be eaten raw for the milky juice of the plants has a bitter taste. Boiling the tender leafy shoots in a change or two of water removes the bitterness. They are then both tasty and wholesome.

Among the Dakotas, the young seed pods, while still firm and tender, were also used as food. These were usually boiled with buffalo meat or venison. Those who have tried them state that they make a most palatable green vegetable, comparable with okra.

The Indians of southern California have made a chewing gum from the milky juice of the milkweed plants. The juice is collected and allowed to stand overnight near a fire. This causes the juice to coagulate, and at the same time its bitter taste disappears. Of course, it doesn't taste like the chewing gums sold in the stores, but the Indians no doubt enjoyed it.

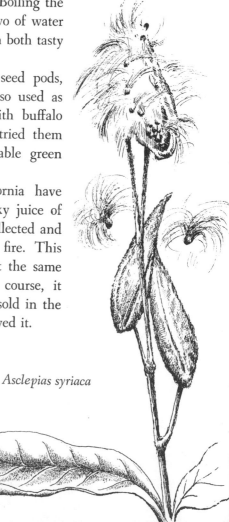

Asclepias syriaca

WILD POTATO-VINE (*Ipomoea pandurata*)

The wild potato-vine is really a close relative of the sweet potato, and both are, in fact, species of morning-glories. It is a trailing or sometimes a climbing vine, and it is often seen in dry fields and along roadsides. All summer, it produces big, trumpetshaped, white flowers with purple centers.

Deep beneath the ground, the potato-vine has an enormous, fleshy, sweet potato-like root which lives from year to year. It may extend from two to three feet down into the earth, and it often weighs from ten to twenty pounds or more.

Some people who have tried the big roots, after they have been roasted, say that they resemble sweet potatoes but have a slightly bitter taste. Others claim that they are hardly fit to eat. The roots were easy to roast in their camp fires, so they were sometimes used as food by the Indians. They may not have been a very choice food, but they were better than nothing when more palatable foods were unavailable or scarce.

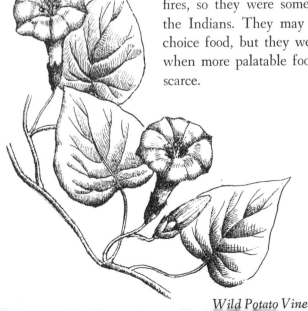

Wild Potato Vine

ELDERS (*Sambucus*)

Sambucus canadensis

Throughout the East, the common elder (*Sambucus canadensis*) is a shrub that is widely found in moist places. It has a rank odor, and its big flat-topped clusters of small white flowers are heavily scented. Most people are quite familiar with it, and every country boy knows that its large-pithed branches are excellent for making whistles.

By late summer or early fall, the flower clusters become big flat-topped clusters of berries, black in color, which are greedily eaten by the birds. They are quite seedy, but they are juicy and fairly sweet, though they still possess some of the rank "eldery" flavor. Most people would hardly consider them as being fit to eat raw, but the Indians seem to have enjoyed them. People in the country, too, have long gathered them for making jelly and pies.

In the West, the fruits of the blue-berried elder (*Sambucus glauca*) were likewise used by both the Indians and the white settlers. Its berries are somewhat larger than those of the eastern elder. They are bluish-black, but are so densely coated with a powdery, white, waxy bloom that they seem to be a bright blue. Many people regard them as the finest of all elderberries for making pies.

VIBURNUMS (*Viburnum*)

Some of the viburnums have edible fruits, and the Indians always gathered them in the fall. They are like very small plums, with a big stone and a thin, sweet, and pleasant-tasting flesh. Most country youngsters have enjoyed nibbling on them at some time or another, and some species are commonly called "wild raisins."

Another viburnum found in Canada and the Northern United States is called the high-bush cranberry. (*Viburnum trilobum*). Like other viburnums, it has fruits with large stones, but the fruits are a bright red and have an acid but pleasant flavor. It grows in many places where the real cranberries are not available, and its fruits are a good substitute when made into a sauce or jelly.

Highbush Cranberry

The Composite Family

The Composite Family

SUNFLOWERS (*Helianthus*)

Sunflowers have long provided the Indians with food. In the Midwest, the big seeds of the common sunflower (*Helianthus annuus*)—which is now the State Flower of Kansas—were always favored because of their large size. This is the sunflower commonly cultivated today both for its huge heads of flowers and for its valuable seeds. It was also cultivated by some of the Indians long before the coming of the white man.

The Indians made many uses of the big seeds of this sunflower. Slightly parched and ground into flour, they were used for making bread and thickening soups. A very fine cooking oil was obtained by boiling the crushed seeds in water, then skimming the oil off the surface. Large quantities of sunflower seeds are grown today for this valuable oil, as well as for poultry and wild-bird feed. One can even buy little packets of the roasted seeds in the stores, and they make delicious nibbling.

Seeds

Helianthus annuus

Another sunflower, which we call the Jerusalem artichoke (*Helianthus tuberosus*), provided the Indians with edible tubers that were cooked like potatoes. It was one of the few wild plants cultivated widely by the Indians, and they probably spread it throughout much of the East. In time it was carried to Europe and grown there. The Italians called it "girasole," a name which sounded very much like "Jerusalem" to the English. That is how this sunflower, a native of America's midwestern prairies, happened to get such a foreign-sounding name.

Helianthus tuberosus

ANGIER, BRADFORD. *Free for the Eating.* The Stackpole Company, Harrisburg, Pa. 1966.

ANGIER, BRADFORD. *More Free-for-the-Eating Wild Foods.* The Stackpole Company, Harrisburg, Pa. 1969.

COON, NELSON. *Using Wayside Plants.* Hearthside Press, N.Y. 1969.

CRAIGHEAD, JOHN J., FRANK C. CRAIGHEAD, and RAY J. DAVIS. *Field Guide to Rocky Mountain Wildflowers.* Houghton Mifflin Co., Boston, Mass. 1963.

FERNALD, MERRITT LYNDON, and ALFRED CHARLES KINSEY. *Edible Wild Plants of Eastern North America.* Idlewild Press, N.Y. 1943.

KIRK, DONALD R. *Wild Edible Plants of the Western United States.* Naturegraph. Healdsburg, Calif. 1970.

MEDSGER, OLIVER PERRY. *Edible Wild Plants.* The Macmillan Co., N.Y. 1940.

Glossary

agave—known also as the century plant. A member of the amaryllis family, native to North America.

American beech—tree of eastern North America, recognized by its smooth, gray bark.

American Nelumbo—also known as the yellow lotus. Has edible, acornlike seeds.

arrowhead—aquatic plant of the *Sagittaria* family, known by its arrowhead-shaped leaves.

arrowroot—tropical American plant, yielding a nutritious starch.

arum—any plant of the genus *Arum*, having a flower which consists of a spike enclosed in a large sheath.

biscuitroot—a low plant, native to the American west, similar to the yampa. Its roots served as food and barter for American Indians.

bitterroot—stemless plant with narrow and fleshy leaves. Grows in Montana and Colorado.

blueberry—the edible berry of a shrub belonging to the heath family of plants—arbutus, azalea, laurel.

brier—a prickly plant or shrub, *i.e.*, greenbrier.

bulrushes—grasslike herb plants with pithy or hollow stems. Found in wet or marshy places.

buttercup—field plant, growing close to the ground. Takes its name from the color and shape of the flower.

butternut—white walnut.

cabbage palmetto—cabbage palm, native to southeastern United States.

camass—member of lily family of plants, having sweet, edible roots. Native to western United States.

caraway—seed of this plant, used in cooking and medicine.

cattail—reedlike marsh plant with long, dense spikes as flowers.

chestnut—tree of the beech family, bearing edible nuts.

chinquapin—shrubby chestnut, native of the United States, with small nuts, each in its own bur.

conifer—cone-bearing evergreen.

corm—the fleshy, bulblike base of the stem of a plant.

cow parsnip—a plant whose stalks spread from a common center such as the carrot, parsley, celery, or parsnip.

cucumber root—a plant of the lily family having a fleshy rootstock with a taste resembling the cucumber.

cycad—the most primitive of existing seed plants bearing a cone in the center of a cluster of palm-like leaves.

elder—member of the honeysuckle family of trees or shrubs, with clusters of white flowers and red, berrylike fruit.

fern—plant characterized by having a few leaves, larger than the stems, with spore sacs on the undersurfaces.

filbert—species of hazelnut.

greenbriers—woody vines with bright green and prickly stems.

groundnut—plants with underground, edible roots—peanuts.

hackberry—tree or shrub, yielding pea-sized, cherrylike fruit. Also known as the sugarberry. Native of North America.

hickory—species of North American tree, yielding a valuable wood and edible nut.

huckleberry—shrub similar to the blueberry.

Indian apple—May apple.

Indian breadroot—native of North America; member of bean family of plants.

Jack-in-the-pulpit—plant of North America, growing in marsh areas, and known for the flowers growing from its club-shaped stalk.

leek—member of the onion family, resembling a large, green, spring onion, and having an onionlike aroma.

lily—any plant of the botanical genus *Lilium,* having showy flowers and a scaly bulb at the base of the stem.

Mariposa lily—member of the lily family; found in western United States and Mexico.

marsh marigold—cowslip; grows in meadows and marshes.

May apple—a perennial herb with yellowish, egg-shaped fruit.

maypop—edible fruit of the passionflower. Native to southern United States.

mesquites—trees or shrubs of southwestern United States and Mexico. Have beanlike pods (often called honeypods), rich in sugar.

milk weed—a family of plants that secretes a milky fluid (latex).

mulberry—fruit of the mulberry tree.

ostrich fern—a tall, North American fern.

palm cabbage—swamp cabbage.

palmetto—a palm tree with fan-shaped leaves.

paloverde—a green-barked, spiny, desert shrub, native to Mexico and southwestern United States.

papaw—the small, fleshy fruit of a bush or small tree of North America.

papaya—tropical American tree, having yellow, melonlike fruit.

passionflower—American climbing vine with pulpy fruit or berry that sometimes can be eaten.

pecan—species of hickory.

persimmon—a fruit tree, having acid, plumlike fruit that sweetens as it ripens.

piñon—pine of Rocky Mountain region, with large, edible seeds.

plantain—tropical plant or tree with broad, flat leaves, and fruit that resembles a banana.

pokeweed—North American plant with purple berries and root used in medicine, and edible shoots resembling asparagus.

ponderosa pine—large pine tree of westen North America, with light, soft wood and yellowish-brown bark. Also called western yellow pine.

pond lily—water lily.

prickly pear—pear-shaped, prickly fruit of the cactus. Also known as Indian fig.

purslane—yellow-flowered, trailing plant, used for salads and herbs.

red mulberry—dark-purpled fruit of the American mulberry.

rootstock—a root-like underground stem sending leafy shoots from the upper surface and the roots downward from the lower side.

saguaro—giant cactus of Arizona.

saw palmetto—dwarfed and scrubby-looking pine with fan-shaped leaves. Grows in Georgia, Florida, and westward to the Mississippi.

saxifrage—an herb. Some grow wild between rocks; others are cultivated for their flowers.

sedge—a rushlike plant that grows in marshy areas.

sego lily—a lily plant with bell-shaped flowers, native of the western United States.

shadberry—berry of the shadbush. Also known as the juneberry.

shadbush—North American shrub, bearing edible berries—the shadberry.

shagbark—a species of hickory.

skunk cabbage—evil-smelling, broad-leaved plant of North America, found in wet ground. Also grows in Japan.

skunkweed—another name for skunk cabbage.

Solomon's-seed —a plant of the lily family, having a thick root with seal-like scars.

snowberry—evergreen shrub of North America, with birch-flavored berries.

spadix—club-shaped stalk of a plant.

spikenard—East Indian plant famous for its aromatic root.

spring beauty—small woodland plants which send up, in early spring, a stem with a pair of fleshy leaves and delicate pink flowers.

squawroot—another name for yampa.

swamp cabbage—bud of cabbage palmetto; resembles a cabbage and can be used for food. Also known as palm cabbage.

tallowwood—a low, spiny tree or shrub growing in central Florida. Also known as the hog plum.

toothwort—small woodland plants of the mustard family which flower in early spring and have mild peppery rootstocks or tubers.

tuber—fleshy outgrowth of an underground stem such as the potato or the radish.

viburnum—a tree or shrub of the snowball family.

wild parsnip—uncultivated parsnip.

wild potato vine—groundnut.

wild rice—a tall grass of northeastern North America that thrives in shallow water. Its grain is used for food.

yampa—related to the caraway plant. Also called squawroot.

About the Author

William Grimm has written several books about plants and trees. A graduate of the University of Pittsburgh, he majored in biological science and education. In Pittsburgh he worked as a park naturalist. He was also a scoutmaster and the official naturalist for the boy scouts there. Later Mr. Grimm was with the Game Commission in Wildlife Research, and helped do a mammal survey of Pennsylvania. He served in the United States Army and taught junior high school for eight years. He now lives in South Carolina.

About the Artist

Ronald Himler has written and illustrated a number of children's books. He was born in Cleveland, Ohio, and received his diploma from the Cleveland Institute of Art. He attended Cranbrook Academy of Art, New York University, and Hunter College. At one time he worked as an industrial sculptor in Research and Development at General Motors Technical Center. He was also a toy sculptor and designer. Mr. Himler lives with his wife and two children in New York City.